EUGÈNE IONESCO

WORLD DRAMATISTS

# EUGÈNE IONESCO

RONALD HAYMAN

WITH HALFTONE ILLUSTRATIONS

FREDERICK UNGAR PUBLISHING CO.
NEW YORK

*First American publication 1976*
*© 1972, 1976 by Ronald Hayman*
*Printed in the United States of America*
*Library of Congress Catalog Card Number 75–10103*
*Designed by Edith Fowler*
*ISBN 0–8044–2388–1*

# CONTENTS

Chronology                                                          1
Interview with Ionesco                                              5
Plays                                                              17
       *The Bald Soprano*        17
       *The Lesson*              26
       *Jacques or Obedience* and
         *The Future Is in Eggs*   33
       *The Chairs*              43
       *Victims of Duty*        61
       *The Motor Show, Maid to Marry,*
         and *The Leader*    71
       *The New Tenant*         75
       *Amédée*                 78
       *The Picture*            85
       *Improvisation*          87
       *The Killer*             91
       *Rhinoceros*            101
       *Frenzy for Two*        113
       *A Stroll in the Air*   115
       *Exit the King*         128
       *Hunger and Thirst*     137

*Killing Game*      148
*Macbett*      160
*The Mire, The Hermit,*
     and *What a Hell of a Mess!*      169
Ionesco's Achievement      185
Stage and Broadcast Productions      189
Notes      195
Bibliography      201
Index      207

# CHRONOLOGY

1912    Born on 26 November at Slatina (not quite
        100 miles west of Bucharest), the son of a
        Romanian lawyer and his French wife.
1914    When he was 18 months old the family
        settled in Paris.
1916    His father left Paris for Bucharest to fight in
        the war. They lost contact with him and
        assumed he had been killed. Mother had to
        work in a factory to support the children.
1921    Developed anemia and sent to live in the
        country in the village of Chapelle-Anthenaise.
1922    Returned to Paris.
1923–4  Discovered literature through reading Flau-
        bert. Started writing plays that would end
        with the children smashing furniture and
        crockery and throwing their parents out of
        the window. Also a patriotic play, poems,
        "memoirs" and a film scenario.
1925    Parents divorced and father given custody of
        both children. Returned to Romania and
        transformed his play into a Romanian patri-

otic play. His father remarried and the new wife drove her stepdaughter out of the house. Eugène stayed till he was seventeen, then ran away.

1929     At Bucharest University studying for a degree in French. Writing poems with "surrealist overtones" influenced by Maeterlinck and Francis Jammes.

1930–5    Published a pamphlet of poems in Romanian and contributed to literary magazines.

1934     Published a collection of literary essays under the title *Na* ("no"). In the first part he attacked the poets Tudor Arghesi and Ion Barbou and the novelist Camil Petrescou, who were then fashionable, only to reinstate them in the second part.

1936     Married a philosophy student, Rodica Burileano. Shortly afterward his mother died.

1938     Received a grant from the French government to come back to write a thesis on "The themes of sin and death in French poetry since Baudelaire."

1939     Returned to Chapelle-Anthenaise. Worked on thesis but found it difficult to write in French. Met Emmanuel Mounier and began reading his books.

1940–3    Lived at Marseilles lecturing on Kafka, Flaubert, Proust, Dostoevsky, etc.

1944     Birth of his daughter, Marie-France.

1944–7    Lived in Paris, correcting proofs for a publisher.

1948     Wrote *The Bald Soprano.*

1950     Wrote *Jacques* and acted in *The Possessed* for Nicolas Bataille at the Théâtre de l'Oeuvre.

1951     Wrote *The Chairs* at about the same time (April–June) as *The Future Is in Eggs.*

1952     While *The Chairs* was playing to empty houses, a defense of the play appeared in the magazine *Arts* signed by Beckett, Adamov, and Raymond Queneau, among others.

Published *Victims of Duty.*

1953   Wrote *The New Tenant* and the story *Oriflamme,* which became the play *Amédée.*

1955   Wrote *Improvisation* and published the story *The Colonel's Photograph.*

1956   A revival of *The Chairs* was made into a success by the intervention of Anouilh, who called it a masterpiece, with black humor à la Molière and "classical" except for the ending.

1957   Wrote *The Killer,* his first full-length play, based on *The Colonel's Photograph.*

1958   Wrote *Rhinoceros.*

1961   Published *Exit the King* in the form of a ballet scenario.

1962   Wrote *Frenzy for Two* (March), *A Stroll in the Air* (summer), and *Exit the King* as a play (November).

1964   Wrote *Hunger and Thirst.*

1970   Elected to the French Academy.

Played in film of his own story *The Mire.*

1973   Published *Macbett.*

Wrote *What a Hell of a Mess!*

# INTERVIEW WITH IONESCO

RONALD HAYMAN: *In* The Bald Soprano *and* The Lesson *you seem to have been writing dialogue without visualizing the room in which the action was taking place. Would it be fair to say that you started thinking about the decor around the time of* Jacques *and* The Chairs?

EUGENE IONESCO: Yes, there was already some visualization in *Jacques*, the third play, and certainly in the following plays. In *Amédée* there is the corpse which grows, and in *The Chairs* it was a visualization of my angst. In the first two plays there was no need for scenery, except for some sort of bourgeois interior for *Soprano*. For me, all that mattered was the dialogue, but then I came to understand that dialogue is only a small part of a play.

*Did the experience of acting in* The Possessed *make much difference to you?*\*

\* After *The Bald Soprano* Ionesco was invited to play Stepan Trofimovich in an adaptation of Dostoevsky's *The Possessed* by Nicolas Bataille and Akakia Viala. It ran at the Théâtre de l'Oeuvre from 4 August 1950 to 18 February 1951.

5

That was very unpleasant.

*Why?*

Because I had the impression of being someone else. An actor needs a certain generosity. He needs to be able to forget himself and lend his own personality to the imaginary character, and I felt alienated. And recently, in September and October of last year (1970) I made a film based on a short story I wrote called *La vase*. I played my own character but even then I felt uncomfortable. I had the impression of being a prisoner of my own character. Acting is a sort of exhibitionism I do not like. I am an exhibitionist but through other people. Perhaps it's hypocrisy or modesty. But modesty is hypocrisy. In any case, I prefer writing for other people to play my lines.

*In the first two plays there is no character with any resemblance at all to you. Then* Amédée *has a little, not very much.*

I don't think so, he's an invented character.

*What about Bérenger?*

Perhaps there's some resemblance there. I spoke to the audience more directly.

*You've cited the distinction Croce made between intuitive thought and discursive thought and you've said that discursive thought should be prevented from intervening in drama . . .*

Croce said that intuitive thought is thought which is specific to literature and art, etc. Art is the expression of intuitive thought and what interested me about Croce is that he provided, perhaps for the first time, a more secure means of knowing whether a work of art is valid or not. He provided a more precise criterion by saying that each time there is something new in the expression—each time there is originality—there's probably merit. The history of art is the history of expression, expression being form and substance at the same time.

*But the way that ideas come into Bérenger's dialogue in plays like* A Stroll in the Air *is very different from the presentation of banal ideas in the early plays.*

Yes, they're plays which give the impression of being more ideological than the others, but it's not the ideology that's important. If you take Pirandello's plays, you see that the psychological theories are very out of date but it's not the ideas that count, it's the passions which the ideas clothe. You can create a very valuable work with a bad ideology, even with banal philosophical ideas. The most important example is Shakespeare himself. His philosophy had been familiar since the time of King Solomon, who said that all is vanity, but what matters is the way the ideas are lived and become flesh and blood.

*Was there any particular reason for dropping the name Bérenger after* A Stroll in the Air?

Just to make a change.

*When did you first get interested in Jarry and 'Pataphysics?* *

Jarry since I was fifteen; 'Pataphysics more recently because it didn't exist—at least not in a visible form—until about 1948 or '50 with the College of 'Pataphysics. But of course 'Pataphysics existed before, it exists now and

---

* 'Pataphysics. See page 121 for definition. The College of 'Pataphysicians was founded by a group of Jarry's admirers after the last war. Members have included Prévert, Queneau, Vian, and Ionesco.

it will exist tomorrow. Everything's 'Pataphysics. What we're saying now is 'Pataphysics.

*Richard Coe said that with* A Stroll in the Air *you moved further away from 'Pataphysics.*

Yes, it's less important for me now, I think. That's 'Pataphysics without 'Pataphysics. I catch myself at the game of message bearing. I have always been against message in literature because I believe, as Nabokov put it, that the writer shouldn't deliver messages because he isn't a mailman. But I notice there are messages in what I wrote, though not the messages that people expect of me. Critics reproach me for not having a social or Marxist or Brechtian message.

*You have a sympathy with Mounier's personalism?**

Yes, to a certain extent. Especially around 1938 when I knew him, there was reason to be afraid of totalitarianism and Mounier's attitude was interesting. To be humane, the individual has to give himself to others. In face of the enemies of humanity, human society preserves its individuality but justifies it socially . . .

*What about Buber and Hasidism?†*

* Emmanuel Mounier (1905–50). From reading Péguy he conceived the idea of a synthesis between Christianity and Socialism. The basic tenet of his personalism was the supremacy of the human person above material necessities and collective systems. What differentiates personalism from individualism is his insistence on the primacy of interpersonal relations. Personal existence, he maintained, is constantly subject to tension between interiorizing and exteriorizing tendencies. To maintain your interiority you have to go outside it. *La personne est un dedans qui a besoin du dehors.* ("The individual is an inside that needs an outside.")

† Martin Buber (1878–1965). Influenced by Kierkegaardian existentialism and anxious to resolve the dualism implicit in essentialist theories of knowledge, he postulated a distinction between I-It relationships, in which the outside world is treated as

That's something quite different. That's my penchant for metaphysics. I don't know whether there are any signs of Buber's influence in my plays.

*There are critics who say you are serious about the ideas of the antiworld that Bérenger puts forward in* A Stroll in the Air.

In physics there is still talk of the antiworld and of antimatter. Heisenberg for example . . .

*In* Fragments of a Journal *you talk a great deal about dreams.*

It isn't the unconscious that dominates in dreams, it's a sharper form of consciousness. Dreaming is a sort of thinking in words and images, and precisely because the external world is no longer there, one can fall back on oneself. It's a moment of meditation. Dreams are always dramas; one is always in a situation. Jung said that the dream is a play in which one is author, actor and audience. It's total theatre.

*But you believe that what is said in dreams is true?*

Certainly consciousness is censored by the unconscious and vice versa. You can have very precise insights in dreams. Things appear in them with great clarity. There's a lot of talk about dreams but we don't trust them. We hear about the dreams of Descartes and it

---

an object, and I-Thou relationships, in which it is confronted as a subject. The "dialogic principle" of I-Thou implies a dialogue between man and God, Buber said. No reciprocal human relationship is possible without confronting the Thou of God.

Buber was influenced by Hasidism, a mystical development of Judaism which began in eighteenth-century Poland. Orthodox adherence to traditional doctrine was leavened by a strong emphasis on divine immanence and an insistence that God must be served through joy. It advocated constant communion with God through thought and prayer.

seems that the French physician Lucien Poincaré invented his theory when he was dreaming. One communes with oneself. Now, with psychoanalysis we interpret dreams but it seems to me that dreams themselves are an interpretation. It can be the truth.

*You prefer Jung to Freud?*

Yes.

*Because he leaves the door open for religion?*

Yes, he doesn't exclude it. He says that it's an imperative need. He makes no religious pronouncements himself but psychologically one needs God and no doubt that corresponds to a certain reality.

*But that doesn't prove that God exists?*

We don't know. That's where the betting begins.

*Already in* The Lesson *the Maid becomes motherly towards the Professor and in several of your plays, from* The Chairs *to* Hunger and Thirst, *the wife seems to be capable of mothering the man.*

She is. By her nature. We are all sons of woman . . .

*The concierge who figures in so many of your plays has been called a symbol of the bourgeoisie.*

Yes. The universal bourgeoisie.

*It is possible to read into* The Lesson—*among other things—a criticism of the conventional educational system.*

You can draw a lesson from anything. Even from a lesson. And you can find things of which the author was not conscious. For me, it was a game—games with words—but perhaps there are some memories, more or less conscious, of the difficulties I had when studying philology. But the purpose is also different . . . This language is empty. It no longer corresponds to anything. A sort of emptiness of language and a refusal of its call to culture. For the Professor words are just means of taking possession of a human being and through all his verbiage and word play, underneath this superficial culture, there is instinctual reality which this language masks or unmasks.

*There's a very interesting connection between the Professor and the Monks in* Hunger *and* Thirst.

Perhaps . . .

*It's sometimes said that your plays are better without intermissions.*

Yes, I've never liked intermissions because I think one should be able to move a play from one point to the next without interruption. There is a sort of progression in my plays which shouldn't be broken. In *The Killer* there was no intermission because it is a very short play, but *Exit the King* lasts one and a half hours without intermission. *Killing Game* lasts two hours or one hour fifty minutes without intermissions. In the eighteenth century the intermission was indispensable. In Racine's plays each act lasts for twenty-five minutes for the simple reason that the candles had to be renewed. And in the nineteenth century there were intermissions because theater was mundane and bourgeois and people needed to see each other and chat as if they were at a party. But the Greeks had no intermissions and the Japanese Noh Theater has no intermissions.

*And in* Hunger *and* Thirst *the intermissions are one of the reasons you constructed the play in the way you did.*

Exactly. Each act was constructed to some extent separately from the others, constituting a little play in itself.

*For instance, it is difficult to see any relationship between Aunt Adelaide in Act One and Brechtoll and Tripp in Act Three.*

Yes, you're right. I think that *Hunger and Thirst* is the only play to have been constructed with a view to intermissions. Certainly one doesn't see the relationship between the three acts and it's a bit like three plays but after the departure from the house it's a sort of quest, which becomes visible in Act Two and is concluded in Act Three. But in my opinion, if you have several intermediate acts, not just one, the play regains a certain unity. I wrote another act to put between the second and third (which would become the fourth).* In the second act it's an amorous quest and in the act I wrote later to be inserted, it's a quest for consciousness, for example. You could have several quests. In fact I think I was a bit influenced by a play like Claudel's *Le soulier de satin*. It's a long quest. The first act and the last act remain as they are, but one could have in between several acts or several scenes. . . .

*You once said that what we need is a new surrealism.*

Yes, certainly, because most of the surrealists have become writers with a message, while others have been more or less suffering from hardening of the arteries. That's to say that automatic writing has become very automatic. The surrealists have got into bad ethical habits. What we need is a new thrust. The barriers need to be broken all over again for the interior world to come out into the open, to demolish the barriers of

---

* *Au pied de la mur.* Published separately as *The Foot of the Wall* in the English edition.

conscience and prejudice. The stream of consciousness has to overflow.

*It's odd that no one before you made surrealism viable in the theater.*

There have been surrealist plays. There was Vitrac and there were plays I do not know by Breton and Soupault. And I think there was even a dadaist play. But surrealism became formalist; the avant garde fell into academicism.

*It was interesting in* Fragments of a Journal *you found five distinct meanings for the word "absurd." I often think that the playwrights of the so called theater of the absurd have very little in common.*

Yes. I find that the name "theater of the absurd" which has been glued on to us is absolutely meaningless. All theater is absurd. Shakespeare makes Macbeth say life is a tale told by an idiot, signifying nothing. It seems to me that there are only two possibilities if you want to write drama which bears on fundamental problems: either it is agnostic, which isn't the same as absurd, or it's religious, like the theater of Claudel. It must say either yes or no to religion. . . .

*In* Notes and Counter Notes *you say that since we don't want to die we must be intended to be immortal.* Yes, I think we should be immortal. That's why we are afraid of dying. We feel that we should be made to be immortal.

*But if mortality is the fundamental fact of human, animal and vegetable existence . . .*

You can accept, you can resign yourself, you can have some faith or other in obeying the rules of what is called nature. But the human condition is inadmissible.

Having to get older, being diminished—it's inadmissible. Having to die is a condition which I reject.

*You say that it's incredible that man has accepted it for centuries but what else is there to do?*

One rejects it uselessly, I admit, but it's a law I won't accept.

*If only there were a way of disobeying it . . .*

Yes.

*You say that since you were young you have had very little contact with the young and especially when you were young yourself.*

Yes. My youth was spent partly in France, partly in Romania, where I saw the hatching of the Nazi movement. At that time everybody was a Nazi just as today everybody is an extreme leftist. If someone said he was a democrat then, he would have been lynched and the best spirits of the time, the intellectuals, were fascists, just as the intellectuals of today are leftists. The banners are different but the fanaticism is the same. Books are even being burned, as in the old days, and there's antisemitism under cover of anti-Zionism. If you are against communism you are against democracy. Anglo-Saxons are detested, just as in the Nazi times. I find that very disquieting. You cannot read *Mein Kampf* today in the way that Mao's little red book is read, but the little red book is even worse than *Mein Kampf*. To me it seems there's a certain diabolical aggressiveness, a fanaticism which just changes its banner.

*I very much like what you've said about politics as being a means of keeping people apart rather than bringing them together.*

Yes, I felt very ill at ease then, in the same way as I do today. Now, as then, there's no friendship among the young, only camaraderie. And camaraderie is finally solitude in common. The world suffers from the fact that people cannot assume the right to be solitary. In the past there were solitaries. Now solitude is a catastrophe, a trauma. But people don't escape into themselves and even if one is with other people who march in rhythm, the fashion is to hide one's own solitude—but without escaping it . . .

*You have said that it's out of fear of death that people kill each other.*

I think it is that. It's to be ahead of death. And then there are other reasons. People detest themselves and they kill themselves in others. They kill the other so as not to have to kill the self. The vitalism we saw earlier in German youth—their *élan vital*—was finally seen to be an enormous collective suicide. There are many reasons for suicide and fear of death is an important one. There are characters in Dostoevsky who were afraid of death but still wanted to kill themselves —perhaps for other reasons too—because they wanted to be free vis-à-vis God—to be stronger than God, not to accept the power of God. Kirilov in *The Possessed* kills himself because life is a sort of death . . .

*In* Hunger and Thirst *you obviously intend Brechtoll to be a representative of left wing totalitarianism and Tripp to be a fascist.*

Yes, but the most exploratory totalitarianism is that of the monks. Brechtoll and Tripp still think. They're ideologues and the dogmas of one neutralize the dogmas of the other, and it all ends by drowning itself in an impersonal totalitarianism which spies on us.

*You have used the word nihilism but surely it isn't nihilistic to insist that neither form of belief is worth dying for?*

Death is unacceptable and the conditions existing in heaven are almost equally unacceptable if our condition is reflected in that of heaven. You feel the malaise everywhere. It is the reason there have been so many social reformers, so many prophets. That's the reason for what is called progress. We are all unsatisfied with our condition and want to change it, so we follow this or that prophet or ideologue or revolutionary . . .

*What is your attitude to existentialism?*

I am not against existentialism. I am against the fact that Sartre, out of hatred for what he calls the bourgeoisie, destroyed documentary evidence he had about Soviet concentration camps. Which was very serious, because he had a great influence at that time. His political behavior was irresponsible, childish, and criminal at the same time.

*But you don't agree with existentialism, do you? You're an essentialist, aren't you?*

Yes. I am not enough of a specialist in philosophy to have precise ideas.

*You have said "Nothing can change what I am but I exist in different fashions."*

I had forgotten what I'd written. One's life changes every two weeks or so and it isn't coherent philosophies I've been presenting but passions and desires. I have found support in one idea and another according to the inclination of the moment. I am agnostic and desperate at not having some faith or other.

The author and publisher wish to thank *Transatlantic Review* for permission to reprint the above interview with Ionesco, which appeared in the August 1971 issue.

# PLAYS

## *The Bald Soprano*

Ionesco was in his thirty-sixth year when he wrote his first play. As a child he had been fascinated by Punch and Judy shows but he never liked the theater, being embarrassed by the physical presence of the actors. It was when he started to teach himself English by copying phrases out of a conversation manual that he became very interested in the clichés he was transcribing and the characters whose conversations they were meant to represent. Mr. and Mrs. Smith and Mr. and Mrs. Martin in *The Bald Soprano* are the same Smiths and Martins who exchanged commonplaces in the *Assimil Manual* and one section of the play was created directly out of their textbook dialogue. If the information they laboriously pass each other is totally redundant—that there are seven days in a week, that the ceiling is above us and the floor below us—then this turns out to be a joke which works on several levels, burlesquing not only the attempts at dramatic dialogue that we find in all such textbooks but also the dialogue of the conventional play in which the maid and the butler or the husband and wife establish a situation for the audience by telling each other what they both know already.

> MRS. SMITH: Goodness! Nine o'clock. This evening for supper we had soup, fish, cold ham and mashed potatoes and a good English salad, and we had English beer to drink. The children drank English water. We had a very good meal this evening. And that's because we are English, because we live in a suburb of London and because our name is Smith.

The dialogue does not remain for long at this level of banality. Two other elements are soon introduced: the nonsensical and the pseudological. Mrs. Smith starts talking about a Romanian grocer who has just arrived from Constantinople, specializing in yogurt. He holds a diploma from a school of yogurticians in Andrinopolis and makes homemade Romanian yogurt in England. She then tells her husband about a doctor who, before operating on a patient's liver, went through the operation himself though there was nothing wrong with his own liver.

> MR. SMITH: Then how was it that the doctor came through it all right and poor old Parker died?
> MRS. SMITH: Why? Because the operation was successful on the doctor and on Parker it wasn't.
> MR. SMITH: In that case, then, Mackenzie's not a good doctor. Either the operation should have been unsuccessful on both of them or both of them should have gone under.
> MRS. SMITH: What do you mean?
> MR. SMITH: Well, if they can't both be cured, a really conscientious doctor ought to die with his patient.

The conversation is now on a different level. Mr. Smith, studying the births, marriages and deaths column in the newspaper, cannot understand why the age is always given of the people who have died but never of the babies who have been born. The clock joins in the confusion by striking seven and immediately contradicting itself by striking three. The confusion of time is developed when Mr. Smith finds in the paper an announcement of the death of a man called Bobby Watson who died, he says, about two years ago. But immediately afterward he is speaking of going to the funeral about eighteen months ago, about the talk there was of his passing away about three years ago and about what a good-looking corpse he was after he had been dead for four years.

The confusion about time soon extends to a confusion about identity. Bobby Watson's wife is also called Bobby Watson.

> As they had the same name, when you saw them together you could never tell one from the other.

And Mr. Smith directly contradicts himself when he describes her.

> She has regular features, but you can't call her beautiful. She's too tall and too well built. Her features are rather irregular, but everyone calls her beautiful. A trifle too short and too slight perhaps.

Next we hear that they are thinking of getting married next spring and next that their two children are both called Bobby Watson. So, apparently, are all their relations.

If there is an amnesia implicit in the Smiths' exchanges of information which is already familiar to them, the Martins who now arrive on the scene are equally amnesiac. Haven't they seen each other before? In Manchester perhaps? Gradually the conversation establishes that they both came down from Manchester on the same train, and traveled in the same carriage, that he put her case up on the rack, that they have both been living in the same street in London, in the same house, on the same floor, in the same apartment, with a two-year-old daughter who has one red eye and one white. So, eventually, after four pages of dialogue, they recognize each other as husband and wife, Donald and Elizabeth. But the Maid, who tells us her name is Sherlock Holmes, contradicts the evidence which has painstakingly been built up.

> The child Donald talked of is not Elizabeth's daughter, not the same child at all. Donald's little girl has one red eye and one white eye just like Elizabeth's little girl. But whereas it's the right eye of Donald's child that's red and the left eye that's white, it's the left eye of Elizabeth's child that's red and the right eye that's white.

When the Smiths and the Martins sit down for a four-handed conversation, a rhythm is established, first in the hesitant H'ms and the silences that come between each brief commonplace, then as Mr. Martin and the Smiths interpolate comments and exclamations in unison during Mrs. Martin's narrative about a man she saw in the street doing up his shoelaces. Mr. Martin then describes to the others how he saw a man in a subway who was reading a newspaper. It was in pointless conversations like this that Ionesco was trying to recreate a feeling he had.

> It's the fact that we do understand one another that I don't understand. If, intentionally, you put

yourself completely outside everything, or one floor
above what's going on, if you look at people as
though they were part of a show and you yourself
were a being from another world looking down
on what's happening here, then you wouldn't
understand anything, words would be hollow,
everything would be empty. You can get this feeling if you block your ears when you're watching
people dancing. What are they doing? What can
it possibly mean? Their movements are senseless.
I write plays to express this feeling of astonishment, this feeling of amazement.[1]

What follows raises the question of whether we are
entitled to assume that incident B will always ensue on
incident A just because it always has in the past. Can
we take it that the sun will rise tomorrow morning just
because it has always risen every morning so far? A
ring at the doorbell is assumed to mean that someone
is at the door waiting to come in, but after three times
going to answer the doorbell and finding no one there,
Mrs. Smith says "I've learned from experience that
when you hear a ring at the doorbell it means that
there's never anybody there." The fourth time she
refuses to answer it and it is Mr. Smith who admits the
Captain of the Fire Brigade, who tells them that although he has been waiting at the front door for about
three-quarters of an hour, it was not he who rang the
doorbell the first two times. Nor was anyone else ringing
it. It was he who rang it the third time and then hid,
as a joke, when Mrs. Smith answered the door. Like
Pinter, though writing much earlier, Ionesco is constructing such a complex fabric of contradictions that
it becomes impossible to reconstruct what "really"
happened, diverting the interest away from the tangles
in the past towards the entangled attempt in the
present to unravel them.

A conversation about fires soon gives way to an exchange of stories—first two surreal fables about animals, like updated La Fontaine, and then two equally nonsensical stories about humans.

A recognition scene between the Maid and the Fire Chief ("I am, in a funny sort of way, her spiritual son") echoes the recognition scene between Mr. and Mrs. Martin at the same time as parodying the traditional recognition scene of the melodramatic plot. But when the Maid recites a repetitious poem called "The Fire", in honor of the Captain, the others push her out of the room. He goes, too, because he will have a fire to attend to in three-quarters of an hour and sixteen minutes exactly.

The conversation of the other four returns to the mixture of banality and inconsequentiality characteristic of Ionesco's borrowings from the conversation manual. ("I can buy a pocketknife for my brother, but you could not buy Ireland for your grandfather.") But soon we reach a point where language breaks down altogether. The tension between the characters, the stage direction says, grows until they are all standing and shouting at each other, raising their fists and ready to hurl themselves at each other's throats. The sounds of the words become as important as the meanings and there is so much nonsensical punning that the English translation is only a very rough equivalent of the original.

> De l'ail à l'eau, du lait à l'ail!

becomes

> Said the barley to the cabbage, said the cabbage to the oats!

and, very oddly indeed,

Khrishnamourti, Khrishnamourti, Khrishnamourti!

becomes

Krishnawallop, Krishnawallop, Krishnawallop!

"At a certain point," Ionesco has said, "I have the feeling that the world too could start running haywire, like a machine."[2] Or as he put it in *Notes and Counter Notes*, "For me, what had happened was a kind of collapse of reality. The words had turned into sounding shells devoid of meaning: the characters too, of course, had been emptied of psychology and the world appeared to me in an unearthly, perhaps its true, light, beyond understanding and governed by arbitrary laws." This does not mean, of course, that it is a play about the impossibility of communicating.

> I wasn't concerned with the impossibility of communication or with solitude. Quite the contrary. I am in favor of solitude. . . . There *is* a degree of communication between people. They talk to one another. They understand one another. That's what is so astounding.[3]

Nor is it helpful to characterize the play, as Richard Coe has characterized the whole of Ionesco's drama, as, "a satire upon the bourgeoisie, its speech, its manners and its morals."[4] As Ionesco himself has said, "There probably was in my plays some criticism of the petite bourgeoisie, but the petite bourgeoisie I had in mind was not a class belonging to any particular society, for the petit bourgeois was for me a type of being that exists in all societies, whether they be called revolutionary or reactionary; for me the petit bourgeois is just a man of slogans, who no longer thinks for himself but repeats the truths that others have impressed upon him ready-made and therefore lifeless. In short, the bourgeois is a manipulated man."[5]

In 1958, in a review of *The Chairs* which triggered off a newspaper controversy in which Ionesco himself, Philip Toynbee and Orson Welles were subsequently to take part, Kenneth Tynan wrote

> Ionesco's is a world of isolated robots, conversing in cartoonstrip balloons of dialogue that are sometimes hilarious, sometimes evocative, and quite often neither, on which occasion they become profoundly tiresome.[6]

The robot element in the characters stems, no doubt, partly from Ionesco's childhood pleasure in Grand Guignol, partly from the hatred he shares with Jarry for the physical presence of actors on the stage, and partly from the view he takes of human society. He emerged on the international scene at a moment when the Brechtian influence was dominant, and the social was becoming widely accepted as the most important dimension to a play. Tynan believed in the possibility of finding social solutions to most human problems; Ionesco did not.

> No society has been able to abolish human sadness, no political system can deliver us from the pain of living, from our fear of death, our thirst for the absolute; it is the human condition that directs the social condition, not vice versa.[7]

With most playwrights, the first play can be shown to embody the preoccupations which shape the whole of their subsequent development. With Ionesco this is not altogether the case. The good-looking corpse that was four years old when it was buried may provide some indication of the obsession with death that is so recurrent in the later plays and it prefigures the gigantic corpse that will not stop growing in *Amédée*. But what is more important is the use of accelerating rhythms which feature again and again in his future work. Ionesco (who is one of his own best critics) has pointed out the resemblance this gives him to Feydeau.

> We all know at least one famous remark of Bergson's, that "the comic is something mechanical encrusted on the living." Feydeau (in *A Flea in Her Ear*) starts out with something living and a very small element of the mechanical; then the mechanical element takes over until there's nothing left but the machine alone, wild, quite out of control. A machine that gets out of control is a machine that works too well, so well that everything is turned into part of the machine; it takes over everything, the whole world gets sucked into its mechanism.[8]

He has also said "I have the feeling that the world too could start running haywire, like a machine."[9] So if his characters start to behave like robots, then they are directly expressing his inner fears about the nature of external reality.

# The Lesson

None of the characters in *The Bald Soprano* are characterized in the normal way: except for a couple of the Maid's speeches and a few of the Fire Chief's, much of the dialogue could equally well be spoken by any one of them. In fact the play ends with Mr. and Mrs. Martin sitting in exactly the same position that Mr. and Mrs. Smith were in at the beginning of the play and speaking exactly the same lines.* In the second play *The Lesson* he does characterize but only

---

* Originally Ionesco had two ideas for an ending. One involved planting two or three actors in the audience to start a row and invade the stage. The theater manager would then come on with some policemen who would open fire on the audience and order the theater to be cleared. The other involved an interruption of the argument between the Smiths and the Martins by the arrival of the author who would end the play by shaking his fist at the audience and shouting abuse. When neither alternative was acceptable he decided to end the play by beginning the play all over again with the Smiths. It was only after several months that he had the idea of substituting the Martins for the Smiths to emphasize the interchangeability of the characters.

in order to reverse the characterization of all three characters as the action proceeds. The eighteen-year-old girl is cheerful and lively at the outset but she becomes more and more morose and sleepy until a nervous aphasia seems to have set in. The Professor starts by being polite and subdued, quickly mastering the prurience that flickers into his behavior three times when she says she is quite ready for him, when he speaks of nibbling her ear away to illustrate the problem of subtraction and when he calls her "sweetie" (*mignonne*). Then as he grows more confident and aggressive, his voice changes and the climax of killing her with an imaginary knife is unmistakably a symbolic rape. Previously thin and piping, his voice becomes "an extremely powerful, braying, sonorous instrument," while her voice, initially resonant, has become almost inaudible. The changes in the Maid's character are equally emphatic. Apologetic and submissive at the start, she becomes masterful enough to strike her master and order him about.

Although Jarry's Père Ubu does not change in this way—the characters were written to be played in masks so none of them could—he possibly stands behind the figure of the Professor. Derived by Jarry from a childhood memory of a tyrannous schoolmaster, he represents very much the same kind of schoolboy image of corrupt and bossy authority. Ionesco has said he hopes *Ubu* was an influence on *Rhinoceros*.

> Ubu is a character who's so simplified that he becomes an archetype, an incarnation of the power and truth of myth. He's dehumanized because he's so human, human in the worst and lowest ways.[1]

In one sense Ionesco has here reverted to the source of Jarry's inspiration—the figure of the bullying master, but undoubtedly the main source for the figure of the Professor was Ionesco's father. In *Présent passé passé présent* he describes how all his hatred for authority, militarism and the dominance of the male over the female stems from memories of his father. "Everything that I've done has been done, as it were, against him."

He was a fascist lawyer who was kept on at the tribunal by the communists when they took over in Bucharest. "My father was not a conscious opportunist —he believed in authority. He respected the state. He believed in the state whatever it was. I didn't like authority, I detested the state, I didn't believe in the state whatever it was."[2] He wanted his son to become a bourgeois—a magistrate, a soldier or a chemical engineer. Ionesco, who consequently hates dogma, whether Brechtian or of any other sort, shows in *The Lesson* how the young girl is weakened by the non-sensical teaching which strengthens the old man.

Like Jarry, Ionesco makes his characters into surreal grotesques by exaggerating absurdly.

> If the essence of the theater lay in magnifying its effects, they had to be magnified still further, underlined and stressed to the maximum. To push drama out of that intermediate zone where it is neither theater nor literature is to restore it to its own domain, to its natural frontiers. It was not for me to conceal the devices of the theater, but rather make them still more evident, deliberately obvious, go all out for caricature and the grotesque, way beyond the pale irony of witty drawing room comedies.[3]

But he is very unlike Jarry in his style of exaggeration and in the pleasure he takes in combining opposites in the same character. The girl does not know the names of the four seasons but she wants to study for all the doctorates; she cannot subtract but she can multiply 3,755,998,251 by 5,162,303,508 in her head. Her stupidity about subtraction becomes almost sympathetic because she is resisting his theorizing, insisting on trusting the evidence of her own senses. He becomes less and less sympathetic as he puffs himself up with pedantic arguments, launching into a nonsensical discourse about Spanish and neo-Spanish, muddling his own categories. He throws in a parenthetical lesson on voice production, which gives the actor freedom to exercise his vocal chords in a demonstration of how to pronounce a selection of words. The dialogue almost becomes a monologue as, ignoring her complaints of toothache,* he tutors her in pronunciation by means of an inconsequential story which is based on the joke of assuming distinctions between sounds that are absolutely identical.

> I had a friend in the regiment, a viscount, who had a rather serious speech defect: he was unable to pronounce the letter "f." Instead of saying "f," he used to say "f." If he wanted to say: fresh fields and pastures new, he would say: fresh fields and pastures new. He pronounced filly as filly; he said Franklin instead of Franklin, fimblerigger instead of fimblerigger, fiddlesticks instead of fiddlesticks, funny face instead of funny face, Fe Fi Fo Fum instead of I smell the blood of an Englishman; Philip instead of Philip; fictory instead of fictory; February instead of February; April-May instead of April-May; Galéries Lafayette and not, as it should be pronounced, Galéries Lafayette; Napoleon instead of Napoleon, etcetera instead

---

* It may not be irrelevant that it was toothache that made Ionesco aware of the beginnings of physical decay in himself. "One tooth goes, then another. A lock of hair, then another. Then a nail, a finger joint, a finger, the hand. . . ." (*Présent passé passé présent*, p. 15.)

of etcetera and so on etc. . . Only he was lucky
enough to be able to conceal the defect so well,
thanks to his choice of hats, that no one ever
noticed it.

From this it is an easy step to the next confusion.

You always have the same meaning, the same
composition, the same structure of sound, not
only in this word, but in all the words you can
conceive, in every language. For each single concept is expressed by one and the same word and its
synonyms, in all the countries of the world.

The sentence he takes as an example

The roses of my grandmother are as yellow as my
grandfather who was born in Asia

is exactly the same, he tells her, in Spanish, and in neo-
Spanish, but when she tries to translate it into both
these languages he accuses her of muddling one with
the other. Translated into Latin and into Italian, he
tells her, the sentence is still exactly the same. The
confusion is very much like that introduced into *The
Bald Soprano* with the family of Watsons who all have
the name Bobby, but here the nonsense is teased out
more elaborately and a refinement is introduced when
he tells her "Italy" is the Italian for neo-Spain. "My
country is neo-Spain" becomes, when translated into
Italian, "My country is Italy." This and the different
names of the capitals are apparently the only differences
between the various languages.

Those who say, for example, in a Latin they take
to be Spanish: "I've got pains in my chilblains,"
are as perfectly well understood by a Frenchman

who doesn't know a word of Spanish as though he were being addressed in his own language. What is more, he believes it is his own language. And the Frenchman will reply in French like this: "I too have got pains in my chilblains," and he'll make himself understood perfectly well by the Spaniard who will be positive the remark was made in the best Spanish.

Finally he produces an imaginary knife, ordering her to pronounce the word "knife" in all the different languages, while staring at it and imagining it to belong to the language she is using. Tired and aching by now all over her body, she obeys listlessly, complaining how piercing his voice is. She becomes more and more distraught and tearful, backing away as he brandishes the invisible knife. The dialogue becomes more rhythmic as he urges her to repeat the word "knife." She obeys, but interpolates the names of various parts of her body, complaining how they are aching. The word "breasts" is pronounced three times before he kills her with the imaginary knife and she falls onto a chair into what Ionesco calls an immodest (*impudique*) position, her legs spread wide. The second thrust of the knife is upward and he is out of breath, trembling all over his body as he finishes.

It is the Maid who now takes charge of the situation, reprimanding him like a strict nurse and knocking him down when he aims a blow at her, too, with the imaginary knife.

> And I gave you proper warning, too, only a little while ago! Arithmetic leads to Philology, and Philology leads to Crime. . . .

But as soon as he has said he is sorry she helps him to get rid of the body. Her boyfriend, the priest, will help.

Like *The Bald Soprano*, the play will end as it began, with the arrival of a new pupil. But the weakest section comes now, just before the end. A perfunctory reference to forty coffins makes the point that the murder we have seen is the fortieth today and when the Professor remarks that he could be arrested if he were found out, the Maid ties a swastika armband around his arm, reassuring him that he has nothing to fear if the killing is political. So suddenly, gratuitously, perversely, an anti-didactic play is given a didactic twist and the invisible knife, which was already under severe strain, being partly phallic and partly a symbol of language made solid, is made to bear the weight of extra associations with fascism. Ionesco may have been wanting to make the point that fascism distorted the language and made it into a weapon but this idea is not organically integrated and there is too much logic in the illogic of the play's structure for a new idea to be introduced so late.

## Jacques or Obedience and
## The Future Is in Eggs

Ionesco wrote the two Jacques plays in 1950 and 1951, though the first, *Jacques or Obedience** was not staged until October 1955 and the sequel *The Future Is in Eggs* not until June 1957.

He had subtitled *The Bald Soprano* "antiplay" and insofar as antitheater is a meaningful category, it is equally valid for all his early plays. As he has said himself, "they were a criticism of the commonplace, a parody of the old-fashioned theater that was no longer theater." The conversation manuals had made him realize that the boulevard theater was populated with hollow men talking a hollow language, and, as he says, "like *The Bald Soprano*, *Jacques* is a kind of parody or caricature of boulevard theater, boulevard theater going bad, going mad."[1]

His definition of the petit bourgeois conformist is "a man who adopts the thought patterns (or the principal ideology) of whatever society he happens to belong to

* Published in the United States as *Jack, or the Submission*.

and stops asking questions."[2] *Jacques* starts out by being
the story of a nonconformist who is bullied by his conformist family into conforming over marriage. Like the
Bobby Watsons, the family is all given the same name
—Jacques Father, Jacques Mother, Jacques Grandfather
and Jacques Grandmother, while his sister is called
Jacqueline. This is partly to underline their conformism, partly because Ionesco does not believe in differ-
entiating between characters. As he told Robert
Kanters[3] in 1960, "I rather disapprove of stressing individual differences when one is creating a character.
What interests me above all is the deep-rooted identity
of people." The consequences of this are twofold: he
creates characters like Bérenger who have an aura of
everyman about them, embodying the yearnings, the
fears and preoccupations Ionesco sees as being common
to us all; he also creates a conformist group like the
families in these two plays and the characters whose
conformism dehumanizes them in *Rhinoceros*. In
*Jacques*, the stage direction's suggestion that all the
characters except Jacques himself could wear masks
would dehumanize them in effect, at the same time as
annihilating character in any conventional sense. But,
as in *The Lesson*, Ionesco still introduces conflicting
characteristics into the same character. The Mother,
for instance, combines benevolence with vindictiveness,
while the malapropisms in the dialogue add to the
confusion.

> I was the one, my boy, who gave you your first
> spanking, not your father over there, who could
> have done it better, he's stronger than me; no, I
> was the one, because I loved you too much. And
> again it was I who made you go without your
> pudding, who kissed you, looked after you, trained
> you and taught you how to emeliorate, to violate,

to articulate, and brought you such nice things to eat, in thingumajugs. I've been more than a mother to you—a bosom pal, a husband, a hussy, a crony, a goose . . . Oh, ungrateful boy, you don't even remember how I used to take you on my lap and pull your pretty little teeth and toenails out. It used to make you caterwaul like a calf, a lovely little calf.

For the first five pages of dialogue Jacques himself does not say a word as the others in turn remonstrate with him in clichés peppered with malapropisms and interrupted by songs from the senile Grandfather. We have no idea what Jacques has done to make them all so angry but his silence exacerbates the situation to the point where his father is threatening to leave. Jacques continues his silence until he is left alone with his sister, who talks nonsense to him, rather as if she were reciting lessons in a grammar class.

I am not an abracchante, he is not an abrac-chante, she is not an abracchante, and you're not an abracchante either.

The climax of the scene comes when she tells him that he is chronometrable. This sends him into a frenzy, the meaning of which can be understood only in the light of what Ionesco has written in his *Fragments of a Journal* about the effects it had on him as a child when he learned he was not going to live for ever. As soon as you know that you are going to die, he says, childhood is over. Childhood is a golden age of ignorance and his own was shattered very early: he became adult at the age of seven. This, of course, is quite irrelevant to Jacques, whose frenzy merely provides a nonsensical turning point. His resistance has been broken and he signals his willingness to conform by announcing

All right, then, yes, yes, so there! I love potatoes in their jackets!

(The French is *pommes au lard* and unfortunately the English translation of *The Future Is in Eggs* is the work of a different translator who makes it into potatoes with bacon. Ionesco says that the translation should be " 'fish and chips'—the banal dish *par excellence*.")

His father now decides not to leave him or to disown him and his mother says they can proceed immediately with the preparations they have already made to marry him. Within seconds, the bride, Roberta, is brought in with her parents, Robert Father and Robert Mother. The reactions of the Jacques family are undignified and dirty-minded: they prod her, sniff her and make lewd gestures, her parents joining in. Her father's description of her is surrealistic:

She's got green pimples on a beige skin, red breasts on a mauve ground; a strawberry navel, a tongue in tomato sauce, shoulder of lamb, and all the beef-steaks required for the kindest regards. What more do you want?

And when her veil is removed we see that she has two noses. Jacques, who had previously accepted her, now rejects her, saying he wants one with at least three noses. His sister warns him about the number of handkerchiefs she would need but he says they would be included in the wedding presents. This is certainly aimed satirically at the petit bourgeois mentality, but the main points are made through the pressure both families are putting on Jacques to get married. The Robert parents obligingly produce a second child who has three noses, Roberta II, who is played by the same actress. When Jacques complains that she is not ugly enough, his family renews its attack on him, with the Robert family joining in. Jacques Father realizes that his son was insincere in saying that he liked jacket potatoes. Both families are outraged but they leave him alone with Roberta II, who, once she realizes that he is not like the others, wins his confidence by telling him a surrealistic fable about guinea pigs.

He now reveals himself as someone who wanted to opt out of life. He was nearly fourteen when he was born, he says, so he realized what life was about and refused to accept the situation. He said so, not to his family, but to the others, who assured him something would be done.

> It wouldn't go on like this, not too long, they promised. As for myself I was to enjoy the highest consideration! . . . To get round me, they took me to see all sorts of meadows and mountains, several oceans . . . maritime, of course, . . . a star in the firmament and two of the better cathedrals. The meadows weren't bad at all . . . I fell into the trap! Everything was faked . . . Oh, how they lied to me. Century after century went by! And the people . . . they all had the word "goodness" on their lips and a bloodstained knife between their teeth. . . .

Now there is no one left to complain to, except the family, who do not understand. And they have barred the way through the attic so there is no escape except through the cellar.

Suddenly she starts talking about herself and telling him a story about a miller who drowned his own new-born baby by mistake for some puppies. She goes on about galloping stallions and he joins in. They share the narrative rhythmically between them and the tempo increases as they grow more excited. A surrealistic visual effect is added—a flaming mane crossing the stage, and they both imitate horses neighing as the galloping rhythm of the dialogue inflames them. Abruptly the rhythm changes as Roberta II meltingly speaks an erotic prose poem.

> In my womb there are ponds and swamps . . . I've a house of clay, where I always feel cool . . . where there's foamy loam . . . and fatty flies, beetles, wood lice and toads. Beneath dripping blankets we make love . . . swelling with bliss! My arms enfold you like snakes; and my soft thighs. . . . You plunge deep and dissolve . . . in the rain of my streaming hair. My mouth is flowing, streaming my legs, streaming my shoulders bare, my hair is flowing, everything flows and streams, the sky's a stream, the stars strow and fleam. . . .

Immediately after this, the cat talk begins. First their dialogue is made to contain as many words as possible beginning with the syllable "cat" and then (after he has taken off the hat he has worn all through the play to reveal that his hair is green) she tells him about her country house where there is only one word for everything—puss.

> JACQUES: To say: bring me some cold spaghetti, some warm lemonade, and no coffee. . . .
> ROBERTA II: Puss, puss, puss, puss, puss, puss, puss, puss

The simplified linguistics of *The Lesson* are taken here to an ultimate. As Ionesco has said,[4] it is an absence of language, nondifferentiation; everything is on the same level, it's the abdication of lucidity, and liberty, when faced with the organic world.

For the frenzied ending of the play, language becomes joined to movement. When Roberta reveals her left hand, which has been hidden, like Jacques's hair, through the bulk of the action, we see there are nine fingers on it, and as soon as Jacques notices this he says he will marry her. "Everything will combine to the revelation of something monstrous," Ionesco said in a working note written in April 1951.[5] "It must do because theater is finally the revelation of the monstrous."

As Jacques clumsily embraces Roberta, kissing each of her three noses in turn, the parents and grandparents silently return, swaying about in a weird dance, surrounding the lovers, silently clapping, pirouetting, or rolling up their trousers. They then continue the dance from a squatting position aimed to embarrass the audience. By the end, before they disappear, they are emitting meows, grunts, and groans.

Though it follows very much the same pattern, the progression towards the final frenetic climax is less effective than it is in *The Bald Soprano*, mainly, I think, because Ionesco has brought himself into the play. Although we do not know until we have read *Fragments of a Journal* and the *Conversations with Eugène Ionesco* just how closely Jacques's desire to opt out from life corresponds to Ionesco's own, it is obvious that Jacques stands out from the family in a more heroic way—however grotesque this heroism is—than we have previously encountered in Ionesco's work. The speech in which he confides in Roberta about his disaffection and tells her how "they"— who they are remains a mystery—made promises to him about what his future life would be like is obviously very significant. It stands out from its context and it announces several motifs which will be developed in several of Ionesco's later plays, but not in this play, which is probably why the speech fails to provide a good point of departure for what is to follow. Roberta has to make what amounts to a new beginning when she starts talking about horses, and the speech about the miller is too much of an irrelevance. The rhythmic galloping they share through the next section of dialogue can be very exciting but the visual effect of the flaming mane is too isolated. Ionesco has not yet learned to make the stage into a medium for creating pictures which amplify the vision and the images of the dialogue. The puss talk is amusing and bizarrely touching even, but the revelations of his green hair and her nine-fingered hand have little but shock value, and the family so has faded out of the action that, although some way had to be found of reintegrating them into the second half of the play, the embarrassing dance is inadequate.

*The Future Is in Eggs or It Takes All Sorts to Make a World* is a shorter play that satirizes breeding in much the same surrealist way that *Jacques* satirizes marriage. When the curtain goes up we find Jacques and Roberta in the same embrace that we left them in at the end of *Jacques*. Absorbed in each other, they are purring and calling each other puss while the families, impatient for offspring, sit around disapprovingly. Three years have gone by but they have been caterwauling at each other all this time, we are told. Jacques Grandfather, who is sitting behind a picture frame like a portrait of himself, has died in the interim, and after potatoes and bacon (that symbol of conformism) have been served and eaten, the news is broken to Jacques, who weeps obligingly when he is ordered to. The rest of the family, more than in *Jacques*, are treated as a chorus, almost like the family in Brecht's *Seven Deadly Sins*. Partly because of the choric factor, more of the dialogue is rhythmic than in *Jacques*, and because the family is kept on stage throughout the action, there is less chance for the play to break up into sections of contrasting textures. Through the eating sequence and a sequence where the news is broken to Jacques, everybody has very short lines and the rhythm is particularly marked when they all surround first the portrait of the dead grandfather and then Jacques himself, condoling by calling out "cordolences" and then congratulating Jacques Mother for slapping her son's face when he gets too worked up.

There is an amusing moment when they all hold their noses as Grandfather steps out of the frame to tell them how he died, but when he is not allowed to sing, he goes back sulkily and stays behind the frame. His death is related to the necessity for regeneration when, led by Jacques Father, they all chorus "Grandfather is dead, long live Grandfather." When Father says "We must assure the continuity of our race," Jacques asks "Why?" But he is given no chance to ventilate his nonconformist doubts as he did in the first play and neither he nor Roberta resists when Roberta's parents lead their daughter away to give her some training in regeneration.

Once again the build-up to the climax follows the same pattern. While Roberta is still offstage with her parents, Jacques starts to cry out with labor pains and she is heard clucking shrilly like a chicken. The parents fuss over them, encouraging them in the same obscene way as in *Jacques* but Jacques's only moment of rebellion comes after he faints. Realizing where he is when he recovers, he distractedly says how much he wants to get away.

Robert Father now comes on with the first basket of eggs and the others, speaking in lines which by their uniform brevity create a sort of rhythm, make Jacques sit on them to hatch them while the *co-cocodacs* from Roberta continue offstage. The movement of the others becomes almost a dance and when Jacques puffs noisily like a steam engine, the rhythm of the puffing escalates, as do the clucking noises from Roberta, while Robert Father and Jacqueline track ceaselessly in and out bringing more and more baskets of eggs, one leaving as the other arrives. The accumulation of eggs we get on stage is the first example of the proliferation which will be so recurrently thematic in Ionesco's work.

The movement, as usual, becomes frantic. As the egg baskets arrive, Jacques Mother pours eggs all over her son and spins around in the center of the stage calling out "Production, production" which, together with "Co-cocodac" and the stylized puffing "Tuff tuff tuff" becomes a chorused refrain, the movement continuing simultaneously. The dialogue, in very short lines, is carried on under the refrains and the tumult, with Jacques Grandfather conducting the action from his frame with an outstretched forefinger. Then dialogue becomes terser and less meaningful as a new refrain, "Yes yes yes," is introduced. There is a moment of suspension when Jacques interrupts the rhythmic affirmations of the others with a reference to pessimists, anarchists, and nihilists, and there is one moment of hopeless pleading.

> I want a fountain of light, incandescent water, fire of ice, snows of fire.

But he is still silenced by the others when their cries of "Production" and "Long live the white race" and the general noise and movement have resumed.

# The Chairs

In the old couple in *The Chairs* Ionesco achieves a far more effective expression of the anguished frustration and the longing for the unobtainable that he tried to achieve in *Jacques*. Jacques is not exactly a heroic figure but the old caretaker and his wife are removed that much further from heroism and the play does not have its fulcrum in a contrast between foreground figures and background figures. Even the contrast between the visible characters and the invisible characters becomes comparatively unimportant. All the characters are functions of the play's image, which is above all an image of nothingness. The theme of the play, as Ionesco has said, is the ontological void.

> I first had the image of chairs, then that of a person bringing chairs as fast as possible on to an empty stage. . . . The chairs remain empty because there's no one there. And at the end, the curtain falls to the accompanying noise of a crowd, while

all there is on the stage is empty chairs, curtains
fluttering in the wind, etc. . . . and there's nothing.
The world doesn't really exist. The subject of the
play was nothingness, not failure. It was total
absence: chairs without people.[1]

But it was this almost Beckettian image of nothingness
which inspired Ionesco to a more imaginative use of the
theater's visual possibilities than he had ever achieved
before. The points are no longer being made entirely
through dialogue and the physical action of the characters. To fill the stage with emptiness he invents an
action in which the dialogue for the first time fuses
perfectly with the changing visual background and the
sound effects.

From the beginning he creates a theatrically meaningful atmosphere. The ninety-four-year-old woman is
lighting a gas lamp, while the ninety-five-year-old man
leans out of the window. They are on an island surrounded by stagnant water, and mosquitoes are coming
in. So there is a relationship between the inside and the
outside which we have never had before in any of the
indeterminate rooms of the previous plays. Here too,
though, the characteristic Ionesco contradictions are
present: he talks of seeing the boats in the sunshine,
she tells him it is night time. When she pulls him away
from the window he sits down on her lap to be fondled
as if he were a child while they talk about what his
life might have been.

> You're so clever, my dear. You might have be-
> come a president general, a general director, or
> even a general physician or a postmaster-general,
> if you'd wanted to, if you'd had just a little
> ambition in life. . . .
> OLD MAN: What good would that have done us?

> We shouldn't have had a better life . . . after
> all, we have a job to do, I am a quartermaster-
> general, since I'm a caretaker.

The characteristic wordplay on "general" distinguishes
this from Uncle Vanya's kind of regretful retrospection
on what life might have been if only it had not been
what it was. They play games like children and argue
like children ("It is," "It isn't") about whether it is
his turn to pretend. And each evening of their seventy-
five years of married life, she has made him tell her the
same story about what happened to them eighty years
ago when they were shut outside a garden. After this
hint of Eden, we get a contradictory hint that the action
is set in the distant future, because she says that Paris
faded away 400,000 years ago. In any case the action
which ensues has nothing to do with any particular
social or historical context.

The old man sitting on the old woman's knee, crying
for his mother, the old woman rocking him in her lap,
soothing and singing to him, saying any old nonsense in
a comfortable tone of voice—all this is touching and
funny at the same time because it penetrates into what
is rudimentary in almost any situation involving a man
and a woman. The man needs his wife-mother to make
him believe that he has something, a message that is
worth passing on to other people, to make him believe
that he is different from the others and has greatness
within him. Instead of aiming outright at embarrassing
the audience, Ionesco is now able to embarrass, move,
and amuse at the same time. The situation is one in
which we cannot but recognize our own weaknesses,
but the extreme grotesqueness of what is happening
with such a very old man and such a very old woman
makes it all the funnier and all the more touching.

OLD MAN: I've a message, you're right, I must fight
for it, a mission, I can give birth to a great idea,
a message for all men, for all mankind . . .

OLD WOMAN: For all mankind, my dear, your
message! . . .

OLD MAN: It's true, that's really true . . .

OLD WOMAN (*blowing the* OLD MAN's *nose and
wiping away his tears*): That's the way! . . .
You're a big boy now, a real soldier, a quarter-
master-general . . .

OLD MAN (*he has got off the* OLD WOMAN's *knees
and is trotting about excitedly*): I'm not like
other people, I've an ideal in life. I may be
clever, as you say, I am quite talented, but
things don't come easily to me.

Richard Coe has said that Ionesco uses rhythm as a
substitute for action, that plays like *A Stroll in the Air*
and *Frenzy for Two* are rooted in a static image or
situation and that the accelerating rhythmic pattern
provides all the dramatic tension that is needed. This is
certainly not true of *The Chairs*, which has a satisfy-
ingly well-shaped action that develops very rapidly.

The opening dialogue planted the suggestion that
someone was coming and now we learn that the Old
Man has engaged a professional orator to convey his
message to the guests they have invited. All the important people, the property owners and the scientists,
the learned and the landed, the bishops, the violinists,
the presidents, the tradesmen, the public buildings, the
penholders, the chromosomes, all have been invited.
As the guests are about to arrive, the old couple's excitement mounts until they are trotting nervously about
the room. Then the doorbell rings. As in *The Bald
Soprano* there is no one there, but this time No One
comes in, an invisible lady. They both make conversation with her and when the Old Man fetches a visible

chair, her absence is effectively intensified. They not only talk to her, they listen, laugh, pick up something she has dropped, and answer her questions. With admirable deftness and precision, she is made to be real and unreal at the same time.

An imperious peal at the doorbell announces the arrival of the second invisible guest, a colonel. The Old Woman lets him kiss her hand and when he is introduced to the invisible lady he is soon making advances at her. This is neatly and amusingly established through the old couple's reactions. Not only is the writing extremely imaginative, a great deal of opportunity is given to the two actors to be creative in their mime, their reactions to their invisible guests and the quick looks they exchange with each other as if they were actually in the presence of two other people.

Now two invisible guests arrive at the same time, a great beauty whom the Old Man has admired all through his life, together with her husband, a photographer who has brought a present for the Old Woman, who is hurriedly bringing chairs. (Ionesco insisted that the part should be played by a young actress, "because her performance has to be a positive gymnastic feat, a real ballet with the chairs.")[2] Next there is a contrapuntal conversation between the Old Man and the Old Woman, standing back to back as he chats to the aging beauty and she to the husband, with frequent remarks to one of the first guests.

Like the characters in *The Lesson*, the Old Woman now undergoes a metamorphosis. (And the metamorphosis of all these characters could be seen as prefiguring the transformation of the human beings into rhinoceroses in *Rhinoceros*.) As the conversation goes on, she becomes coquettish, lifting her skirts to reveal a petticoat full of holes, standing with her legs apart, exposing her breasts, laughing and coming out with

erotic cries. The Old Man is becoming sexier but in a
more romantic way.

> May I play Tristan to your Isolde? Beauty lies
> in the heart

Variety, too, is being provided in the dialogue because
the Old Man and the Old Woman are now ignoring
each other completely.

Next they sit down at either end of a row of six
chairs, their four invisible guests between them for a
sequence which is mostly silent. They are saying only
the occasional yes or no as their guests do most of the
talking, inaudibly. When they do start talking again,
they contradict each other without addressing each
other. She tells the photographer that their son ran
away when he was seven; he is saying that they never
had any children. The guilt they both feel is made to
come through in this conversation. According to her,
their little boy accused them of killing all the birds, of
making the sky red with blood; he is saying that he left
his mother to die in a ditch. Both confessional speeches
are comparable to Jacques's confessional speech to
Roberta II. But neither of these stand out at all awk-
wardly. They balance and counterbalance each other
well, while the fact of their being addressed to invisible
characters acts almost as a Brechtian alienation effect.

After a brief sequence of very fragmented sentences,
things start to speed up. Several guests arrive at the
same time and the Old Woman hurries in and out,
grumbling as she fetches more chairs. Journalists arrive,
but the Old Man, flustered at having to look after
so many guests, has no time to give interviews. The bell
keeps ringing and he rushes about talking to different guests, welcoming newcomers, hustling the Old
Woman, introducing her to new arrivals, complaining

about two children that one of the guests has brought, while she, between rushing in with chairs and out again to fetch more, fusses him about whether he put his pullover on. Both move busily about as if the stage were crowded with people and the theatrical effect can be extremely compelling. They grow breathless and exhausted as their movements become faster and faster, and they grow more and more harrassed as they weave their way through an imaginary crowd, which is becoming more and more dense. The speeches become briefer and briefer, the rings at the doorbell and the bumping of boats against the dock more and more frequent—a frenetic climax of the same kind as we have seen in the other plays but, because there are only two characters to create the pandemonium, much funnier. By the time their manic movement stops, we have the impression that the stage is overflowing with people. She now starts selling programs. He talks to some friends among the audience, summarizing a few of his ideas which will be explained fully by the Orator.

> The person and the individual are one and the same person. . . . I am not myself, I am someone else. I am the one in the other. . . . Sometimes I wake up to find absolute silence around me. That's what I mean by the sphere. It's complete in itself. However, one has to be careful. The whole shape may suddenly disappear. There are holes it escapes through.

The light, which has been growing more intense all through this, has reached its brightest when a fanfare and a loud noise announce the arrival of the Emperor, who is also invisible. Hardly able to see him or to get to him through the milling crowd of invisible guests, the old couple obsequiously protest their devotion to him, which leads to a plaintive reprise of the theme of what the Old Man's life might have been—developed this time in terms of the difference that the Emperor's support could have made to his chances.

> My life has been full of suffering. . . . I could really have *been* someone, if only I could have counted on Your Majesty's support . . . I have no one behind me. . . . it would all have been too late, if you hadn't come . . . you are, Sire, my last hope in life. . . .

On one level the Emperor's presence in the room is imaginary and the speech an expression of a lifelong daydream; but on another, the invisible Emperor is no less real than the Old Man: both characters are trembling equally on the verge of the void. The Old Man's belief in his wasted potentiality for greatness keeps reminding us of Vanya but the language is much more generalizing. The mixture of grievance and self-justification in what he says underlines what he has in common with the mute, inglorious Milton inside every one of us. Without being at all realistic, the dialogue accurately reflects what people really feel, though most of the time pride or inhibition or resignation prevent them from coming out with it. Not only does he still believe in his own greatness, after ninety-five years of disappointment, but he still believes in the possibility that he could have saved mankind, if only mankind had listened. Even now he still has hope. The Orator, who has the gift of speech which the Old Man lacks, will deliver the message and the Emperor will listen.

Having blown up this balloon, Ionesco pricks at it with a suggestion of abnormally tardy development in the Old Man. At the age of forty he still used to sit on his father's lap before he went to bed but his hair was already turning grey while his father's was still brown. And here the same preoccupation that figures in *Jacques* breaks to the surface: the Old Man too was married off by his family, who wanted to prove to him that he was not still a child. (The inconsistency of this new information with what we have previously inferred —that he has been married since he was twenty—would not worry Ionesco.) So his wife had to be mother and father to him—which connects with the sequence at the beginning of the play when we saw him sitting on her lap.

The scene is now set for the arrival of the Orator. While he wants the invisible guests to seem as real as possible, Ionesco wants the Orator, who is visible, to be as unreal as possible. He is dressed like a nineteenth-century artist and his movements have something robot-like about them. Introducing him and the message he is about to deliver, the Old Man announces that his wife and he have nothing more to ask of life. He thanks her, rather in the manner of an after-dinner speech, for all she has done for him. Now they are separated from each other by the tightly packed crowd and they will never come together again because they have decided to die both at the same moment by throwing themselves into the water. But before that, we hear another fanfare and see a brilliant flash of light as they throw confetti and streamers over the invisible Emperor, the impassive Orator and the empty chairs. They then jump. We hear their bodies strike the water.

The play ends, not with the anticlimactic revelation that the Orator is dumb, but with real sounds from the invisible crowd and a murmuring of wind and water that

> should be heard for a very long time as though coming from nothing, coming from the void. Thus the audience will not be tempted into giving the

easiest explanation of the play, the wrong one. They must not be able to say, for example, that the old couple are mad or in their dotage and suffering from hallucinations; neither must they be able to say that the invisible characters are only the old couple's remorse and memories. This may perhaps be true up to a point, but it has absolutely no importance; the interest lies elsewhere. . . . So these sounds, this intangible presence, should still be there for them, the audience, even after the departure of the three visible characters and quite independent of the old couple's madness. The tightly packed crowd of nonexistent beings should acquire an entirely objective existence of their own.[3]

He has explained the ending in terms of de Nerval's *Promenades et souvenirs:*

The world is a desert. Peopled by phantoms with plaintive voices, it whispers love songs over the gaping ruins of my emptiness! But gentle ghosts, return!
It could perhaps be that without the gentleness.[4]

*Rhinoceros* at the Longacre Theatre, New York, January, 1961, with Zero Mostel as John and Eli Wallach as Bérenger.

*Les chaises* (*The Chairs*), a revival at the Studio des Champs Elysées, Paris, February, 1956, with Jacques Mauclair as the Old Man and Tsilla Chelton as the Old Woman.

*Victimes du devoir* (*Victims of Duty*), a revival at the
Théâtre de Poche-Montparnasse, Paris, May, 1965,
with Chantal Darget as La dame and Suzanne Flon
as Madeleine.
AGENCE DE PRESSE BERNAND, PARIS

The world première of *Fussgänger der Luft* (*A Stroll in the Air*) at the Schauspielhaus, Düsseldorf, December, 1962.
GERMAN INFORMATION CENTER, NEW YORK

*Le roi se meurt* (*Exit the King*), a revival at the Théâtre de L'Athenée, Paris, December, 1966, with Jacques Mauclair as Bérenger, Christianne Desbois as Marie, and Tsilla Chelton as Marguerite.

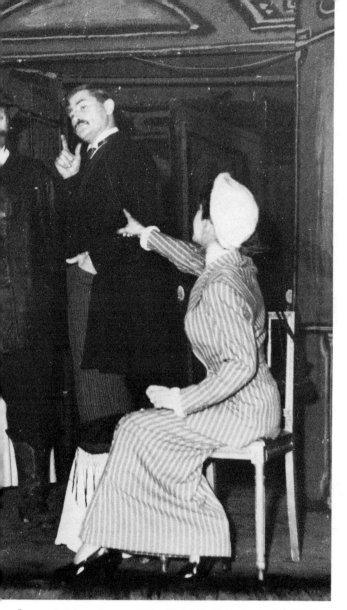

*La cantatrice chauve* (*The Bald Soprano*) at the Théâtre de la Huchette, Paris, October, 1952, with Nicholas Bataille as M. Martin (seated at left).

*Exit the King* at the Royal Court Theatre, London, August, 1963, with Sir Alec Guinness as Bérenger.
SANDRA   LOUSADA,   LONDON

## Victims of Duty

Ionesco was not going to find it easy to go on achieving the same richness of texture he did in *The Chairs*. His next play, *Victims of Duty*, was not finished until fifteen months later (whereas *The Lesson*, the two Jacques plays and *The Chairs* had all been written within the space of less than two years.) *Victims of Duty* was the first of the five plays which he first wrote in the form of a short story. "A Victim of Duty" is a very short short story, less than ten pages, told, like the other four, in the first person. It contains all the main incidents that will be used in the play, from the appearance of the policeman to his murder by Nicolas. But each phase of the action leads far more rapidly into the next. The one moment in the story which is quite unlike anything in the play comes when the policeman penetrates right inside the narrator's thoughts. Ransacking his brains for facts about the former tenant of the apartment, he recalls that sometimes the man used the name Montbéliard.

The narrator does not, apparently, speak the name out loud but the policeman—also without saying anything out loud—confirms he did have the surname Montbéliard. The whole sequence of dredging up memories from the past will become quite different in the process of being theatricalized.

There are also several sections of the play where the movement becomes very leisurely. It opens with a rather desultory conversation, which begins quite promisingly by establishing a contrast between two perspectives—the cosmic and the local—as Choubert tells his wife about different news items in the papers: comets and neighbors being fined for letting their dogs foul the sidewalks. But what follows has nothing to do with this contrast of perspectives. There is some amusing if generalized satire on the ineffectiveness of politicians and the law; then they talk about the theater. Plays have never been anything but thrillers, he tells her. A minute later the Detective makes his entrance.

Again we are to see a deliberate discontinuity in characterization. The Detective, initially soft-spoken and excessively shy, will soon become boorish and domineering. At first he is tentative about troubling them, reluctant even to come inside the apartment, but within minutes he is bullying Choubert to marshall his memories of Mallot, the previous tenant, demanding coffee and addressing Madeleine by her christian name.

He forces Choubert to go back into his own past while Madeleine, who has disappeared to make the coffee, changes as much as the Detective, reappearing as a different woman, with a different walk, a different, more musical voice and a low-cut dress. A siren now, she lures Choubert sexily, obscenely, back into his past. Her arm becomes an imaginary handrail and he moves as if he were going down a staircase. She sides with the Detective when he tries to make Choubert go still deeper down into the mud. Madeleine, wrapped in a shawl with her back to the audience, suddenly becomes an old woman, which cues a speech that is something like a prose poem but less inspired than the equivalent speech in *Jacques*, more verbal and flowery than the equivalent sequences in *The Chairs*.

> When did it happen? Why didn't we stop it? This morning our path was strewn with flowers. The sky was drenched in sunshine. Your laughter rang clear. Our clothes were brand new, and we were surrounded by friends. Nobody had died and you'd never shed a tear. Suddenly it was winter and now ours is an empty road. Where are all the others? In their graves, by the roadside. I want our happiness back again, we've been robbed and despoiled. Oh, when will the light be blue again? Madeleine, you must believe me, I swear, it wasn't I who made you old! No . . . I won't have it, I don't believe it, love is always young, love never dies. *I* haven't changed.

Then to belie his own speech, he turns his back to the audience and holding her hand, tries to skip about with her as they both sing in old, cracked voices. The Detective interrupts, bullying him to go further, further. Mud is a recurrent image as Choubert, groaning with effort, mimes a descent. He moves as if walking with great difficulty on the bed of the ocean.

Here, as in *The Chairs*, Ionesco has made enormous demands on his actors, not at all treating them like marionettes as he tended to in *The Bald Soprano*. And from the later scene, where Choubert has to climb, Ionesco learned from both the actor R. J. Chauffard and from the original director, Jacques Mauclair. The connection between Chauffard's imagination and the physical effort he was making as he first crawled under the table, then climbed on top of it, then on to a chair that had been put on the table, led Ionesco to comment "You really felt he was climbing a steep mountain. This is one of the fairly rare moments when I've understood what the theater is, what it ought to be: a real, living experience, not just the illustration of a text."[1] But it is striking how close this method of staging the sequence is to a scene in a play by Ionesco's *bête noir*, Brecht. In the last scene of *Puntila*, Herr Puntila and Matti climb the Hatelmaberg by constructing the mountain out of tables and chairs. This is only one example of theatrical effects that result from a certain similarity between Brecht's inventiveness and Ionesco's, however dissimilar their plays are in structure, purpose and mood.

A nostalgia for the irretrievable past is a recurrent mood in Ionesco, and in *Victims of Duty* the theme dictates the form of dramatic expression. In *The Chairs* the atmosphere first depended on the sense of place and later on the imaginary counterpoint between the invisible crowd and the empty chairs, their only visible counterpart. In *Victims of Duty* the room is as indeterminate as in the early plays, but the combination of Ionesco's dialogue with the actors' movements can make the imaginary mud far more a palpable presence than the carpet or the walls. The physical environment fades to insignificance.

This is characteristic of Ionesco's method of externalizing internal landscape. Speaking about the painter Gerard Schneider's methods of transforming the reality that surrounded him he said:

> You have only to look into yourself, never outwards; and then to exteriorize, to give expression to what is inside you, what you have seen and heard there, and allow it free play. In this way it

is the world itself, as it is, you will succeed in revealing, authentically, whereas if you only looked outside yourself, you would merely get confused, alienate both aspects of reality and make it incomprehensible to others and to yourself.[2]

Mud is a very important feature in Ionesco's landscape, as Claude Bonnefoy has noticed.[3] He pointed out a connection between the way the characters in *The Bald Soprano* founder in their own language with Roberta's phrase in *Jacques* about being "bogged in," with the sinking into the mud, representing the descent into the past, in *Victims of Duty*, with the drownings in the pond in *The Killer* and with the fear of being sucked down into the mud in the story called "Mud" in *The Colonel's Photograph*.[4] Equally connected with the imagery of mud is the imagery of weight, which Ionesco associates with death, depression, anxiety, despair.

Moi-même je me sentais redevenir lourd, épais, de plomb, une chose en plomb que le vide peut ronger.[5]

(I felt myself becoming heavy again, thick, leaden, a thing of lead that can be eaten away by the void.)

The opposite feeling is represented by an imagery of weightlessness. This of course relates to the flying that features in *Amédée* and *A Stroll in the Air*. The main root of all this imagery was an almost mystical experience that occurred when Ionesco was seventeen or eighteen.

It was in June, around midday. I was walking down one of the streets in this very quiet town. Suddenly it seemed to me that the world was both retreating and moving closer at the same time, or rather that the world had moved away from me, that I was in another world more mine than the old one, and infinitely more light; the dogs in the courtyards were barking as I passed by in the street, but it was as though their barking had suddenly become melodious, or fainter, as if it were muffled; it seemed to me that the sky had become extremely dense, that the light was almost palpable, that the houses had a brightness I had never seen before. . . . At that moment, I said to myself "I'm not afraid of death any more." It felt like an absolute, a definitive truth. I told myself that later on when I was sad or worried, I would need only to remember this moment to discover joy and serenity again. It sustained me for a long time. . . . It seemed to me there was no longer such a thing as weight. I could walk with great steps, with huge leaps, without getting tired. And then, suddenly, the world became itself again, and it still is, or almost. . . . The world has fallen back into a hole.[6]

Elevation, whether achieved by climbing or flying, is often juxtaposed with the opposite experience of sinking down into the depressive mud. Choubert's experience of moving first downward and then upward provides the first clear instance of this. First the journey downwards becomes an imaginary return to childhood and as in *The Chairs* the wife takes the place of the mother. He also makes the Detective into a father substitute and the Detective accepts the projection. Either his recorded voice or, as in the original Paris production, his real voice—once again Ionesco offers an alternative—speaks the father's apologia for his life. His hard luck story in some ways resembles that of the Old Man in *The Chairs* but there is much more emphasis on destruction, which is linked with the im-

pulse to opt out of the only kind of existence that is
available.

> I met nothing but disappointment. The good I
> did turned into evil, but the evil done to me never
> turned into good. Later I was a soldier, I was com-
> pelled, ordered to join in the massacre of tens of
> thousands of enemy soldiers, of whole com-
> munities of old men, women and children. Then
> the town where I was born, with all its suburbs,
> was utterly destroyed. In peacetime the misery
> went on, and I had a horror of mankind. I planned
> all kinds of horrible revenge. I loathed the earth,
> the sun and its satellites. I longed to go into
> voluntary exile, to another universe. But there is
> no other.

His son was born just as he was planning, either in
fantasy or reality, to blow up the planet. The child renewed his feeling of contact with humanity but grew
up to despise him, and just as Choubert is being made
to feel guilty about this, the Detective snaps back into
his own character, urging his victim to devote the whole
of his mental resources to the missing Mallot.

Soon the actor-audience relationship has surfaced into
the action, so preoccupied was Ionesco at this time with
the theatrical situation. Madeleine and the Detective
become theatergoers, with dialogue which keeps cutting
across Choubert's, who is performing on a small stage.
This device works like an alienation effect and enables
Ionesco to satirize the language he is putting into
Choubert's mouth.

> CHOUBERT (*as before*): . . . a magic garden, a
> bubbling spring and fountains and flowers of
> fire in the night . . .

MADELEINE: And I bet you he thinks he's a poet!
A lot of bad Parnassian symbolic surrealism.

CHOUBERT (*as before*): . . . a palace of icy flames,
glowing statues and incandescent seas, continents blazing in the night, in oceans of snow!

MADELEINE: He's an old ham! It's ridiculous! Un-
thinkable! He's a liar!

But only part of Choubert's imaginary journey is staged
on this little platform. For the upward part of the
journey which starts now, mountain imagery comes into
the dialogue. The painfulness of the ascent is suggested
effectively by the language which almost compels the
director to some such staging as Mauclair used.

CHOUBERT: I'm clinging to the stones, I'm slipping
and clutching at thorns, crawling on all fours
. . . Oh, the altitude's too much for me . . .
Why do I always have to climb mountains . . .
Why am I always the one who's made to do the
impossible . . .

MADELEINE (*to* DETECTIVE): The impossible . . .
He said it himself. (*To* CHOUBERT): You ought
to be ashamed.

DETECTIVE: Don't stop now to wipe your brow.
You can do that later. Later. Go on up.

CHOUBERT: So tired . . .

But despite the pressure, Ionesco took time to link the
motif of ascent with the motif of solitude. Choubert
comments on his loneliness and wishes he had a son.
He reaches the point where he can see right through
the sky. Here, like Ionesco in his quasi-mystical experience, he has no fear of death and Madeleine is
frightened of losing contact with him. Entreating him
to come back, she changes character again, becoming
a beggarwoman.

Think about us. It's not good to be alone. You
can't leave us . . . Have pity, pity! (*She is a beggarwoman*) I've no bread for my children, I've got
four children. My husband's in prison. I'm just
out of hospital. I'm sure you've a kind heart.
Sir. . . .


The Detective, realizing he is driving Choubert too far,
joins Madeleine in trying to lure him back by talking of
the solidarity of the human race and reminding him of
the advantages of everyday life. They speak of gold,
fruit, the satisfactions of revenge, the possibilities of
worldly advancement, the beautiful weather—gradually
becoming more and more farcical in their persuasions.
Ignoring them, he bathes in the light until suddenly
the stage is totally dark. When the lights come up he
is sprawling in a big waste paper basket and a new
character, a Lady, is on stage, taking no notice of the
others. Madeleine joins the Detective in pulling and
abusing her husband until another new character comes
in, Nicolas d'Eu (an untranslatable pun on the French
for Nicholas II). Madeleine fetches coffee for him and
Ionesco's favorite theme of proliferation is very amusingly developed with the coffee cups. Vaguely counting
how many people there are in the room, she keeps coming out and going back with more coffee cups until the
whole sideboard is covered. Meanwhile the Detective,
who is talking of plugging the gaps in Choubert's
memory, produces a stale old breadcrust from his briefcase which Choubert has to eat. Nicolas tries to engage
the Detective in a conversation about the theater, while
Choubert obediently chews his crust, making his mouth
bleed.

The proliferation of the coffee cups is becoming more
frenetic as Madeleine's movements become faster and
more mechanical. We are building towards another

characteristic climax. But all through the Detective's harsh orders to Choubert, Choubert's painful complaints, the conversation about the theater, Madeleine's hectic movements in and out with coffee cups, the strange Lady remains passive and silent. The Detective's indifference to Choubert's pain is reminiscent of the Professor's indifference to his pupil's toothache in *The Lesson* and Choubert is similarly broken down by ruthless authoritarianism until he becomes almost like a child again. His character is changed and when Nicolas intervenes to defend him, the Detective's character changes too. Suddenly he is weak and obsequious. This does not prevent Nicolas from working himself up very quickly into a towering fury, at the climax of which he produces a knife to strike at the Detective, who dies asking for posthumous decoration and proclaiming himself a victim of duty.

Now it is Nicolas's turn to change in character. He becomes just like the Detective he has killed, ordering Choubert to chew and swallow the hard bread. Madeleine joins in, ordering both Choubert and Nicolas to chew and swallow, and finally the Lady joins in. As the curtain falls all four of them are ordering each other to chew and swallow.

## The Motor Show, Maid to Marry, and The Leader

*The Motor Show*, which was first produced as a radio play in 1952, is one of the most richly textured of the earlier sketches that have survived. Seven of them were staged by Jacques Polieri in a single "Spectacle Ionesco" at the Théâtre Huchette in August 1953, but three of them—*Les grandes chaleurs* ("the great heat"), *Les connaissez-vous?* ("do you know them?"), and *Le rhume onirique* ("the dream cold")—have been lost. Only *La nièce-épouse* ("the niece-wife") has been published.[1] The farmyard sound effects that open *The Motor Show* set up an antithesis with the title and there is a pleasantly surreal inconsequentiality in the opening dialogue between the Young Lady and the Gentleman who wants to buy a car. She offers him grammar lessons, a standing committee of nine directors, and one sitting hen, and finally introduces the Salesman who inquires whether the Gentleman wants a male or a female car. When he is invited to pinch the cars, we hear first a trumpet, then a neigh, followed by other unlikely sound effects as he tries other cars. The dialogue introduces pseudotechnical vocabulary: turgiodyfractors, pneumonic circulation, and allusions to logic. When the Salesman offers to introduce a young blond vehicle, it is the Young Lady; and when the Gentleman says he will be pleased to buy her, she tells him to put her headlamps on and they can get married at once.

*Maid to Marry* starts with an exchange of platitudes between a boring, middle-aged couple who talk proudly about the Lady's daughter. As though Ionesco gets bored with their conversation, he introduces surreal anomalies into it.

> GENTLEMAN: What's it all leading to? . . . Today human life is the only thing that's cheap!
> LADY: Oh . . . I do so agree with that! . . . Now that's very true . . . You're perfectly right there . . .
> GENTLEMAN: There are earthquakes, accidents, cars and all sorts of other vehicles like airplanes, social sickness, voluntary suicide, the atom bomb . . .

There is more comedy in the way the Lady agrees with each of the Gentleman's remarks, even when he contradicts something he has just said. The main comic point is made by the appearance of the much praised daughter who turns out to be a man in a grey suit with a bushy black moustache.

*The Leader* is a satire on the mass hysteria that demagogues inspire. The device of representing the crowd of admirers by two people, an Announcer, and the sound of cheering off stage works as a powerful alienation effect. By making part of the action invisible

—as in *The Chairs*—though this time by the more straightforward device of having things going on off stage, Ionesco brings out the full absurdity of the crowd's idolization of its hero.

Into this situation he introduces the comedy of a pair of lovers who at first almost miss their chance with each other by obeying the rules of politeness. Their initial formality with each other is reminiscent of the Martins in *The Bald Soprano* but a sudden declaration of love is followed by a decision to marry as abrupt as that in *The Motor Show*. After this they make several very brief appearances, which are interwoven with those of the other three characters, the Announcer and the two Admirers, but as in *The Chairs* the complexity of the movements on and off stage help to give the impression of a multiplicity of characters. The comedy of the commentary on what the Leader is doing offstage depends partly on the introduction of anomalies rather less surreal than those in *The Motor Show*.

> He's dancing, with the hedgehog in his hand. He's embracing his dancer. Hurrah! Hurrah! (*Cries are heard in the wings*) He's being photographed, with his dancer on one hand and his hedgehog on the other . . . He greets the crowd . . . He spits a tremendous distance.

Enthusiastic narrative like this is accompanied by exaggerated outbursts of adoration from the Announcer and the Admirers and the dialogue leads to a crescendo of physical action as the Lovers chase each other while "the crowd" tries to catch up with its Leader. When he finally appears on stage, he turns out to have no head. The stage direction is that the actor who plays the Leader should wear an overcoat with the collar turned up so that nothing else is visible under his hat. In the revival of the sketch by Jean Rougerie Company in *Inédits Ionesco*, the Leader was represented by a hat suspended on a wire with nothing at all underneath it. In either case Ionesco's point about mass leadership is clear enough.

# The New Tenant

*Jacques* has been made into a ballet and *Exit the King* was first published in the form of a ballet scenario, but *The New Tenant*, which has never been adapted, might be more effective as a ballet or a mime than as a play. Its weakness is that the dialogue is almost completely superfluous to the statement that is being made visually through the action. One key sequence is written to be performed in dumb show as the two Furniture Movers bring more and more furniture into the room and the space surrounding the Gentleman gets smaller and smaller. Visually the relationship to *The Chairs* is clear. Space is often one of the main protagonists in Ionesco's drama and in both plays furniture proliferates in much the same way as the eggs in *The Future Is in Eggs* and the coffee cups in *Victims of Duty*, but with the result that the main characters are crowded out.

Between the Gentleman and the Furniture Movers very little dialogue is needed. What matters is his instructions to them about where to put the furniture and these are mostly conveyed by gesture. The main action does not start until the furniture is brought in but far the greater part of the dialogue is in the scene between the Gentleman and the Caretaker, which is really nothing more than a distended preamble. There was a concierge mentioned in *Victims of Duty*, but this is the first one to appear in Ionesco's play and she is quite his most garrulous character so far. Nor is there much point theatrically to her chatter, which is only very mildly amusing. It is just words that are proliferating here and Ionesco seems unable to regulate their flow. The climax of the scene comes when the Gentleman tells her that he does not want her to look after him and the stream of professed goodwill turns into abuse.

Possibly the germ for the main action derives from a childhood memory of a move into a house in Rue Madame, which is near the Rue de Sèvres. The Ionesco family often moved, and this time when the wardrobes were moved in, the staircase was blocked. In the play it is not merely the staircase but the yard and the street outside that get blocked. Traffic comes to a standstill all over the town. Even the subways have stopped; the furniture is cluttering up the whole country. Or so we are told by the Furniture Movers. Here, more clearly than in any play so far, Ionesco is using the stage like a painter to develop a visual idea three-dimensionally and to carry it beyond the framework of the proscenium arch by verbal elaboration. We do not need to see the traffic being stopped; it is enough to see the furniture piling up on the stage and the Gentleman being more and more tightly encircled. In the end the ceiling opens for the final pieces to be brought in and the Gentleman is completely immured.

The stage direction asks for the set, the furniture and

the style of acting to be completely realistic. There are several unrealistic jokes, as when it costs both Furniture Movers a big physical effort to move a vase or a tiny stool and no apparent effort to carry very much heavier pieces. The characteristic acceleration of the action also leads to some unrealistic effects when the folding doors open of their own accord and the sideboard slides on to the stage followed by other heavy furniture, with no apparent help from any human agency.

There is also something dreamlike about the whole progression. The two huge pictures of the Gentleman's ancestors take possession of the back wall. A picture representing a winter landscape is hung over the window with its back facing into the room. The radio is acceptable to the Gentleman only because it does not work. The accelerating proliferation of furniture and the blocking of all available space culminates when the Gentleman, sitting with his hat on, asks for the light to be turned out. The bourgeois interior is no longer the background as it was in Ibsen, it has spread like a wilderness into the foreground, extinguishing the protagonist.

## Amédée

The basic idea in *Amédée or How to Get Rid of It*, the first full-length play, is a very good one and characteristic of Ionesco, though curiously enough it is prefigured in "The Burial of the Dead," the first section of T. S. Eliot's *The Waste Land*.

That corpse you planted last year in your garden. Has it begun to sprout? Will it bloom this year?[1]

The corpse in the apartment of Amédée, a petit bourgeois dramatist, has already grown to be enormous and it is still growing. The visual possibilities this offers are considerable and Ionesco exploits them splendidly. But, as in *The New Tenant*, he has some difficulty in tailoring the dialogue to fit the physical action, and certainly he does not have enough substance for the three-act play he is determined to write. As he has said himself,

As the characters are there, no longer knowing
what to do, they talk, they say anything that comes
into their heads. From the second half of the
second act, you can tell that I'm more or less
treading water.[2]

*Amédée* is the second of the five plays which Ionesco
first wrote in short-story form. In *Oriflamme*, the story
version, it is chiefly lassitude that has made the narrator
let ten years go by without telling the police about the
dead body or getting rid of it. He tells us quite ex-
plicitly that it is the body of a young man who took
advantage of his absence from home one evening to
become his wife's lover. The presence of the corpse,
which is upsetting, actually reflects the disturbance in
the relationship between the husband and wife. If
only they loved each other enough, he tells her, it
wouldn't matter. And he reminds her of what life was
like when they were in love, when the universe was only
a transparent veil with a bright light shining through
it, when the light penetrated them like gentle heat,
when the world was weightless and they themselves
felt light, happy, and astonished at the fact of existence.
But the dead body is a mute witness of a past that has
not always been pleasant. When the narrator finally
gets rid of it, dragging it out of the window by its
hair, he feels as though he were dragging the weight
of the whole apartment or tearing out his own insides
through his mouth. But once outside the apartment,
the corpse becomes weightless and, winding itself
around the narrator's body like a ribbon, it buoys him
up into the air. People in the street and watching out
of windows all applaud delightedly, all except Madeleine, his wife, who tells him that he is rising, but not
in her estimation.

Clearly the early part of the story would be much easier to put on the stage than the end. Until Act Two there is no explanation of how the young man met his death. The first Act elaborates on the inconveniences of having an outsize corpse in one's home. We hear the voices of the concierge and neighbors outside, but Amédée and Madeleine never ask anyone into the apartment. When they cannot prevent the postman from coming in, they panic-strickenly tell him that the letter must be for some other Amédée Buccinioni and that there must be lots of other houses that have the same address. The proliferation of indoor mushrooms is another inconvenient by-product of the presence of the corpse, and there is a variety of theatrical effects to be got out of its growth, which continues during the action. After a loud crash of breaking glass, we hear that its head has gone through the window, and after a variety of cracking and banging noises, we see a huge pair of feet bursting the poor open and sliding into the room.

As in *The New Tenant*, the progression can be seen in terms of an invasion which causes loss of space and loss of freedom. When the curtain goes up on Act Two we see more furniture onstage because the corpse is now taking up more space in the offstage room. But there is more to it than this. As in *The Waste Land*, the corpse comes to symbolize the impossibility of burying the past, and the guilt which accumulates. As Ionesco has said:

> I see the corpse as transgression, original sin. The growing corpse is time.[3]

This theme is developed in Act Two. The movement of Act One is more physical than psychological and it builds towards the same accelerando of physical action characteristic of the climaxes in the one-act plays.

Madeleine has no job in the short story; in the play
she operates a switchboard which is situated in the
apartment, though she puts on her hat before she goes
over to it. The fragmentary conversations she has with
a variety of callers are counterpointed very amusingly
with what Amédée says to himself as he works on his
play.

> Hallo, I'm putting you through. (*Another call,
> another line*) No, sir, there are no gas chambers
> left, not since the last war . . . You'd better wait
> for the next one. . . .
> AMEDEE (*still at the table, to* MADELEINE): Made-
> leine, I can't think of the next line. . . .
> MADELEINE (*to* AMEDEE): Can't you see I'm busy?
> . . . (*Buzz*) Hallo . . . I'm sorry, the firemen are
> away on Thursdays, it's their day off, they take
> their children out for a walk . . . But I didn't
> say today was Thursday. (*Another buzz*) Yes
> . . . Hallo . . . I'm putting you through . . .
> AMEDEE (*standing up, his hand still on the table*):
> Oh, how tiring it is to write, I feel worn out! . . .
> MADELEINE (*as before, answering another call*):
> Yes . . . you wish to speak to his wife? . . . You
> don't mind if she takes it from the bathroom?

This sequence in itself is working up to a climax as the
calls come faster and faster, and at the end of the act
the switchboard starts buzzing again just as Amédée
and Madeleine are having to cope with the crisis of
the feet that have burst through the door and advance
further into the room as they watch.

Besides taking advantage of the intermission to have
furniture brought onstage, Ionesco uses it to make the
legs grow longer and to introduce giant mushrooms.
The feet keep jerking forwards as the new act begins
and Amédée keeps measuring. This is amusing but

much of the domestic bickering between Amédée and Madeleine is uneconomically written. Certainly they are more fully characterized than any previous couple in Ionesco, but the argument establishing Amédée's lassitude and the build-up to his decision to get rid of the corpse are labored. Nor is the revelation of how the man was killed at all useful when it comes; it might have been better to leave this ambiguous, as it was in Act One. There is still some ambiguity—more than there was in the short story—for Amédée says he has no memory of killing him and there is much stress on his absent-mindedness. The presence of the corpse is also linked with the guilt he feels about failing to save a woman from drowning, and Madeleine speaks about the dead weight of wasted years. But all this is already sufficiently present in the play; explicit discussion of it only has the effect of padding.

The continuation of their discussion about the time when they were in love leads to a sequence rather reminiscent of *Victims of Duty*, in which Amédée is pulling images from the past towards him with an invisible rope. We are then given a dialogue between a much younger Amédée and a much younger Madeleine, Ionesco characteristically leaving it open whether the parts should be played by the same two actors or two younger actors who closely resemble them. The woman resists the journey into the past but their argument echoes the short story images of light and weightlessness. The lament at the cruelty of time becomes steadily more lyrical until Ionesco is writing in assonances. Amédée speaks of their happiness in a house of glass, a house of light; Madeleine says it was a house of brass, house of night. (*Maison de verre, de lumière; maison de fer, de nuit.*)

When we cut abruptly back into the more prosaic present, we find Amédée making the point the narrator made in the story—that if they loved each other enough, none of this would have mattered. More realistically, Madeleine insists that love cannot get rid of a corpse. This triggers his decision to take action at last and move the body. But before the action sequence when the decision is put into effect, there are imaginative sequences in which the corpse emits music and green light while continuing to grow so rapidly that they keep having to rearrange the furniture around his limbs. Ionesco wants almost acrobatic movement as they clamber between the giant feet, the door, and the bulky furniture, just as the Furniture Movers in *The New Tenant* had to be almost acrobatic in their maneuvering of furniture on the over-full stage, and as the Old Woman in *The Chairs* had to be extremely agile in moving chairs around.

There is no equivalent in the play to the section in the short story where the narrator finds that dragging the body out of the apartment is like tearing out his own insides. All Amédée can say, before he starts moving the corpse, is that he will be quite sorry to see him go. When the moment comes, Madeleine is practical, urging him to hurry up, while he grows lyrical at the beauty of the night sky. The giant mushrooms, which have not stopped growing, are by now giving off a greenish tint. So if it exploits the contrast between the interior of the apartment and the skyscape visible through the open window, the stage picture should be able to keep pace with the verbal scene painting. But the business of removing the body needs to be staged with considerable ingenuity if the climax of this act is to match that of the first.

Having got Amédée and the dead man's legs into the street for Act Three—the trunk and head are still in the apartment—Ionesco flounders, having very little idea of what to do with them. The American soldiers and the brothel they frequent have nothing to do with the main action. They are mentioned in the story, but only in passing. In the play a drunken Military Policeman is ejected from the brothel bar, shouting for a girl, and there is some comedy in Amédée's conversation with him, trying to speak English. But this inevitably loses point when all the dialogue has been translated into English. The American does not understand when Amédée speaks to him in French about the play he is writing, attacking nihilism and announcing a new form of humanism, more enlightened than the old. Helping him to pull at the body, the soldier has the idea of spinning Amédée round like a top so that the elongated corpse coils round his waist until, as in the story, it has the effect of buoying him up into the air. It opens like a parachute, the head becoming like a glowing banner. To orchestrate the effect, Ionesco introduces policemen who are trying to catch Amédée, girls and soldiers who are enjoying the fun, pyrotechnic effects in the night sky, and people watching out of windows. Certainly the final tableau as Amédée becomes airborne can be spectacular and highly unusual. But except in so far as it depicts the act of casting off the dead weight of the past, it does not have much meaning in relation to the main part of the play. Amédée is apologetic about flying away. He cannot help it, he tells them, and, rather like the Old Man in *The Chairs*, he talks of having wanted to take the weight of the world on his shoulders. The play ends as Madeleine lets herself be persuaded to join the drinkers at the bar and a woman calls from a window:

Let's close the shutters, Eugène, the show's over!

# The Picture

The Large Gentleman in *The Picture* has been described by Leonard Pronko as "a kind of incarnation of Ubu as a businessman."[1] The most garrulous character since the Caretaker in *The New Tenant*, he blows his own trumpet in very much the same way. In his conversation with the Painter, he rambles on about the virtues of hard work, reminiscing sentimentally about how hard the struggle has been. As with the Caretaker, the tediousness of what is almost a monologue is not altogether in focus or sufficiently braced by comedy. It is mildly amusing when the Painter, told to sit down and to put his picture down, can find no chair and nowhere to put it, and like the Lady in *Maid to Marry* he agrees with everything the Large Gentleman says, even when he contradicts himself, as he often does.

He has never married, we gather, and after talking at boring length about his ugly one-armed sister, he suddenly inquires about the price of the picture that he still has not seen. After beating the Painter down from 400,000 francs to 400, he tells him off for his clumsiness in treading on his own picture, which turns out to be very large indeed as he spreads it out on the floor. As he helps the one-armed sister to hang it, the Large Gentleman bullies both of them. Talking about art, he pontificates, rather like the Professor in *The Lesson*, in a mixture of platitudes and nonsense. He also asks for changes to be made in the picture: the Queen should have a crown, her legs should be visible, and so on. By the time the Painter goes, he has agreed to pay the Large Gentleman for the privilege of leaving the picture on his wall.

Now Alice, the sister, abruptly changes character, rather in the manner of the characters in *The Lesson* and *Victims of Duty*. As she becomes stronger, the Large Gentleman becomes weaker. She tells him off severely for buying pictures of nude women and orders him to start work on his contracts. He adds up his profits, which come to 800 million. Hearing from her loud snoring that Alice is asleep in the kitchen, he talks rhapsodically to the picture, climbing up the ladder to kiss it. He also tries to put a three-dimensional crown on the two-dimensional queen. When Alice throws water over him to cool his ardor, he threatens her with a pistol, and when he fires it at her, her wig and spectacles fall off, revealing that she has the same hair, face, eyes and bosom as the woman in the picture. Her missing arm grows back and her stick becomes a sceptre. A neighbor who calls on them thinks the Large Gentleman has been buying statues of queens. He has become an artist, and when the Painter comes back he is told to become a businessman.

# Improvisation

The French title *L'improvisation de l'Alma*
is a reference to Molière's *L'improvisation de Versailles*
and Giraudoux's *L'improvisation de Paris*. Like Molière,
Ionesco makes himself into a character in the play,
which is a satire on the critics who have written as if
they knew better than he how he ought to be writing.
Bartholomeus I, II and III represent Roland Barthes,
Bernard Dort, and Jean-Jacques Gauthier. In fact much
of the dialogue is made up of quotations lifted directly
from their articles in *Théâtre Populaire*, *Bref*, and *Le
Figaro*. Bartholomeus I lectures Ionesco about costumology, Bartholomeus II about historicizing and decor-
ology, Bartholomeus III about audience psychology.

Bartholomeus I tries to persuade Ionesco to finish his
new play quickly so that it can be given scientific treatment in a new theater with scientific actors and a
scientific director. The play is to be a tragic farce about
a shepherd Ionesco saw embracing a chameleon (hence
the full title, *Improvisation or the Shepherd's Chameleon*). To Bartholomeus I it seems to illustrate the

reconciliation of the self with the other and he wants this interpretation to dictate the construction of the play. As Ionesco is no scholar he has no right to have ideas himself.

When he starts reading his play to Bartholomeus I, we find it begins in exactly the same way as the play we are watching. The reading is interrupted by the arrival of Bartholomeus II, whose opening dialogue with Ionesco is exactly the same as Bartholomeus I's, and then by the arrival of Bartholomeus III with whom the same dialogue is repeated once again, only more rapidly.

All three Bartholomeuses wear scholar's gowns; all three combine pedantry with stupidity. They attack Molière, and Bartholomeus I argues that only the ephemeral is of lasting value. Jointly deciding that Ionesco's thinking is tainted, they combine to cross-question him, but soon they are arguing among themselves and the argument very soon turns into clowning.

> BART I (*to* IONESCO): Quiet. (*To* BART III):
> You're thinking tautologically! The theatrical
> resides in the antitheatrical and vice-versa . . .
> vice-versa . . . vice-versa . . .
> BART II: Veecee-verso . . . Veecee-verso . . . Vee-
> cee-verso!
> BART III: Veecee-verso? Oh not veecee-verso, it's
> versa-vircee.

But the three of them seem to be agreed that a theatrical event should have educational value; a playwright should be a schoolmaster. This idea is one of Ionesco's *bêtes noirs,* so their desire to turn the theater into a place for learning is elaborated on at some length.

Carried away by their resounding truisms about the nature of the theater, they do not want to admit

Ionesco's cleaner until he persuades them to let her in so that she can represent the audience. But before she is admitted they must arrange the set, they say; and what follows is an outright attack on Brecht. After opening "the treatise of the great Doctor Bertholus" they put up a sign that reads "A Playwright's Education." This is to "draw the public's attention to the fundamental epic attitude enshrined in each tableau . . . To make it clear that the place is not a real one . . ." They want props that will characterize the historical situation they are expected to pass judgment on.

Turning their attention next to costumology they ask Ionesco to be a walnut so that they can be nutologists. They recostume him, but in exactly the same way. Then they put an extra pair of trousers on him, labeling him with signs saying "Poet" and "Scientist." They now order him to alienate himself when the cleaner comes in—not to be himself. Immediately before her entrance, the action accelerates. He brays like an ass and, gamboling about wearing dunce's caps, they join in.

The cleaner is like the Maid in *The Lesson* in being called Marie and in being the embodiment of common sense. She tells the learned doctors off for being such fools, threatens them with her broom, tears down the labels, drives off all three visitors, and slaps Ionesco twice on the face to bring him to his senses. He ends the play by addressing the audience directly, saying the texts from the doctors' own works have been used in the dialogue so he is not to blame if the audience has been bored. He accuses the three Bartholomeuses of discovering elementary truths and dressing them up in such exaggerated length that they seem to have gone mad. Truths are dangerous, he says, when they take on the appearance of dogma. The critics should describe not prescribe. Finally he makes a statement of his credo.

As I am not alone in the world, as each one of us, in the depths of his being, is at the same time everyone else, my dreams and desires, my anguish and my obsessions do not belong to myself alone; they are a part of the heritage of my ancestors, a very ancient deposit to which all mankind may lay claim. It is this which, surpassing the superficial diversity of men, brings them together and constitutes our deepest fellowship, a universal language.

Seeing that he is taking himself too seriously, Ionesco makes Marie steal up behind the character Ionesco and dress him in one of the scholar's gowns. But we wish she had interrupted him a moment or two sooner.

# The Killer

In *The Killer*, his second full-length play, and the first of the four in which the hero is called Bérenger, Ionesco makes his first major attempt to fuse public and political themes with themes dredged up from levels of personal experience. The radiant city in which the action opens is a clear reference to Le Corbusier's *ville radieuse* and the whole problem of improving the communal happiness through architecture and town planning. But Kafkaesque undertones are soon introduced. Bérenger had difficulty in finding his way into this part of the city, though the Architect tells him that all the trams come this way: it is the depot. There is more than a suggestion of totalitarianism in the files that the authorities keep on all the citizens. It is sinister, as well as being both amusing and theatrically convenient, that the Architect is also a doctor and also the chief of police. This also makes it all the more ominous when he says that he knew Bérenger was on his way to see him, though Bérenger himself had not planned his visit.

What Bérenger says about there being nothing more real than a mirage has its coefficient in the actual construction of the play: an outline of an ornamental pool is made to materialize at the back of the stage, but the Architect is oddly reluctant to let Bérenger look at it, and when he agrees to look instead at the flowering hawthorn, the pool vanishes. So the physical framework of the action is designed to express Bérenger's basic hunger for an external world which reflects the internal.

The Bérenger who feels this hunger is not at all a heroic figure. He represents a combination of Ionesco's private preoccupations and the generalized petit bourgeois. He is righteously outraged with the authorities for resigning themselves so readily to being unable to catch the Killer who is terrorizing the radiant city and he does more than his mere duty as a citizen towards catching the Killer himself, but in the confrontation with him that forms the climax of the whole play, Bérenger becomes impotent. He can neither produce any cogent argument to prove that killing is wrong nor can he bring himself to shoot the Killer, who is only armed with a knife.

In many ways the atmosphere is more dreamlike than in previous plays. Certainly the flying in *Amédée* had its origin in Ionesco's dreams of flying and the giant corpse originated in a dream he had about a dead body spread along the corridor of an apartment he was living in, but in *The Killer* a nightmarish confusion pervades the whole action, from the visit to the radiant city to the confrontation with the Killer. Nothing has hard outlines; things flow into one another. Even in the most overtly political sequences the basic image is oneiric: Mother Peep, who keeps the public geese, is asking the crowd to vote for her. In the geese we may see allusions both to the goose-step and to the geese who saved Rome by waking the guards. But the flavor of the scene is dreamlike.

There is also a dreamlike fluidity in the narrative progression. After the Architect has said he has to be at his office, he goes offstage to come back with a table, offering to divide his attention between his files and Bérenger if he agrees to go on talking. (This is rather like Madeleine in *Amédée* putting on her hat to go to a switchboard on the other side of the room and what the Architect says into the telephone he carries in his pocket is interwoven with Bérenger's dialogue in much the same way as Madeleine's and Amédée's lines are interwoven in the switchboard sequence.)

Bérenger talks about his dreams, saying that the Architect's work has translated them into reality and, aptly, as Bérenger speaks about the real houses and stones and bricks and cement, Ionesco makes him put his hand out to touch empty space. Bérenger's proposal of marriage to Dany, the Architect's blonde secretary, immediately on meeting her, is equally dreamlike, and so is her ambiguous refusal to answer.

When Bérenger and the Architect walk through the invisible gates of the radiant city, the lighting becomes much greyer. The change of locale is also suggested by traffic noises and a few shop signs and advertisements. Then suddenly, as the sign of a bistro lights up and the owner brings on a table, they are sitting inside the bistro. The fluidity of movement from one locale to another is no greater than in that of Arthur Miller's *Death of a Salesman* (1949) but Ionesco's fusion of social statement and private nightmare is different from Miller's: more subjective, less structured. But both playwrights succeeded in exploiting the limitations of the stage (as compared with the cinema) to emphasize the nightmarish instability of the world inside the hero's mind. In *Death of a Salesman* it may be the pressure of a commercial society that has unbalanced Willy Loman's mind but there is no doubt about the reality of the circumambient world. In *The Killer*, the world itself is dreamlike and the unlikely way in which the murderer lures his victims to the pool where he kills them by offering to show them the Colonel's photograph is characteristic of the whole environment.

Certainly the private world of the emotions is fully implicated in the tolerance of the civic authorities.

> Do you know the things that happen in the world, awful things, in our town, terrible things, you can't imagine . . . quite near here . . . comparatively close . . . morally speaking it's actually here! (*He strikes his breast.*)

The nightmarish policemen we see in Act Three emphasize what there is in common between the inner world and the outer. An immensely tall policeman hits people over the head with a stick, while another policeman is too busy directing traffic to pay any attention to Bérenger, who has information which could help them to find the Killer. There is another dreamlike scenic effect as the trucks that have been blocking the road magically move back to let Bérenger through. The traffic policeman vanishes with the back wall and the trucks; suddenly, the buildings in the prefecture become visible in the long avenue in the distance as a miniature streetcar crosses the stage.

Then it is twilight. Bérenger is utterly alone in a desolate road somewhere between the town and the country, with a red sun glowing at the back of the stage. His growing anxiety shows as he walks. Apprehensively he keeps glancing all around him but he is still unprepared for the appearance of the Killer. This encounter produces a final climax which, unlike the end of *Amédée*, is a worthy culmination both to the act and to the whole play.

It is characteristic of Ionesco that he lets the director choose whether the Killer should appear or merely be heard chuckling. If we are to see him, he should be small, puny and one-eyed; probably it is better that he should be invisible. In either case Bérenger's one-sided conversation with him, punctuated by chuckles, is nightmarishly effective.

Bérenger's growing consciousness of his own powerlessness now that he is faced, as he has long wanted to be, with the Killer, is extremely frightening. And by pitching the whole play between dream and reality, Ionesco has built up excellently to this scene, which is very real without being at all realistic. In *Notes and Counter Notes* Ionesco complains that realism, whether socialist or not, never looks beyond reality, that it leaves out of account the obsessive truths that are most fundamental to us. Here he brings us rivetingly close to them.

The oneiric element is less pronounced in the short-story version. *The Colonel's Photograph* is about the same length as *Oriflamme* (twenty-two pages of large print in the French text), but unlike *Oriflamme* the story is in every way inferior to the play. Except for the abortive love story—which in the play gives Bérenger a stronger motive for wanting to track down the Killer when the blonde secretary becomes one of his victims —the story contains all the main incidents of the play but none of them is developed. *Oriflamme* is more than a mere scenario for an unwritten play; *The Colonel's Photograph* is not.

One point which comes out very clearly at the beginning of both the story and the play is the extent to which the fantasy of the radiant city represents a hunger for a virgin world. In *Présent passé passé présent* Ionesco has made the rather Jungian remark that communism cannot be understood without the myth of paradise; the revolution that would unleash pent up energies would be aimed at the rediscovery of purity. The emphasis of the first paragraphs of the story is on the whiteness of the houses, the small gardens surrounding them, the trees flanking the wide streets, the newness of the polished cars, the purity of the blue light in the sky. The play develops this theme. When it starts the light is grey, we hear wind and streetcars, perhaps see a dead leaf fluttering across the stage. Then suddenly, against the dense vivid blue of the sky we have nothing but intense white light on the empty stage. Ionesco asks for a minute of silence in which the emptiness, the blue, the white and the peacefulness make their impact on the audience. Then Bérenger is there, telling the Architect that it is a miracle, and going on to rhapsodize about the lawn, the flowers, the brightness of it all. In the district where Bérenger lives it is so damp inside the houses that it seems to be raining indoors; in the radiant city it never rains at all. There is a special greenhouse with storms inside it for flowers that like wintry conditions. The whole area is an island, the Architect says, with concealed ventilators copied from oases in the desert. This cues Bérenger's line "It's one of those cities that are also called mirages" —which suggests that the whole action we are watching is, on one level, a fantasy. But there are also lines which suggest a very hard shell of totalitarianism around the life which looks so beautiful to us. If the state keeps files on every citizen it is unlikely to allow them much liberty, and the Architect rapidly grows impatient when Bérenger speaks lyrically about his soul.

I'm not capable of judging. It's not one of my
duties. The logic department sees to that.

Later, when Bérenger is trying euphorically to describe the five or six semimystical experiences of brightness he has had—rather like Ionesco's experience of
when he was about seventeen—the Architect is hardly
listening. He is talking angrily over the telephone to
the girl who wants to quit his service. We also hear that
people are wanting to move out of the radiant city but
this is not, as we might have expected, because of any
lack of liberty or of an antilife attitude on the part of
the authorities, it is because people are terrified of the
Killer. Similarly, in the conversation in the bistro, no
attempt is made to distinguish between those evils which
can be blamed on the state and those which are in-
herent to the human condition. Starvation and mis-
carriages of justice are lumped (by the Architect)
together with erosion, death and floods. Ionesco is not
one of the dramatists who write in order to inaugurate
or encourage the kind of social change that can be
brought about by reform.

It would have been easy to let the balance of the play
be disturbed by the thriller element in it, by the tension of the murders and the excitement of tracking down
the Killer. Ionesco creates a mystery by establishing
the point that nobody who works for the civil service
is attacked. This prepares for the murder of Dany, the
blonde secretary who has just left the service, but this
is kept very much to the margin of the play. We hear
a cry and the sounds of a body falling into the water,
followed by a noise of alarmed voices and the screaming
brakes of police cars. But all this is offstage; onstage we
only have Bérenger's distress when he hears the news,
which is counterpointed against the indifference of the

Architect-Police Superintendent, who declares the case closed with the crime unsolved.

In contrast to the uncluttered decor for Act One, Act Two has a realistic set representing Bérenger's room complete with furniture, writing implements, wall hangings and so on. There is some superfluous dialogue at the beginning of the scene with the offstage voice of another concierge who sings a nonsense song and chats at unnecessary length about life with an unseen man. We also hear the offstage voices of schoolchildren, for no apparent reason. Generally this act is less tightly constructed and less successful than either the first or third. A good deal of space is devoted to dragging a red herring across the trail. The behavior of Bérenger's friend Edouard, draws a considerable amount of suspicion on him. He chokes over his rum when Bérenger starts talking about the crime. He seems exaggeratedly indifferent about the murders and extremely anxious to prevent Bérenger from seeing the contents of his bulging briefcase. When it spills open, Bérenger finds enormous photographs of the Colonel in it, together with candies, money, children's watches, and a cardboard box that contains another cardboard box that contains another, and so on. The smallest of them contains the criminal's visiting cards, his address, a photograph of him, an address book with entries in it for all his victims, a diary containing a detailed confession, and a map showing his plans for the future. The only explanation that the unnaturally vague Edouard can give for having all this in his possession is that it was sent to him for publication in a literary journal. When Bérenger insists they must hand over all this evidence to the police, Eduoard first seems reluctant and then contrives to leave the briefcase behind. His attitude is never explained, even when he is cleared of suspicion. We could assume that he is suffering from the same kind of inertia that stopped Amédée from telling the police about the dead body in his flat but Edouard's behavior is too obviously contrived to provide tension in Act Two.

Act Three opens with the Mother Peep episode. Her election promises are highly unattractive and the voices from the crowd which sing out her praises are reminiscent of the cheerleading Announcer in *The Leader*. She talks of teaching her geese to do the goose-step, and when a drunk from the crowd speaks up to say that science and art have done more to change thinking than politics—a point Ionesco would endorse—she sets her geese on him and he is liquidated. After some comedy over two other briefcases which Bérenger mistakes for Edouard's, and after the episode with the traffic and the policemen, we come to Bérenger's encounter with the murderer.

This is a very long soliloquy broken only by chuckles from the Killer. If the director accepts the option of making the Killer invisible, the audience will have the option of thinking that Bérenger is talking to himself, to the discrepancies in his own nature which his conscious humanism cannot master. He starts off confidently, knowing that physically he is much the stronger man. Sententiously he lectures the Killer about the desecration of other people's happiness. But he soon falls into the trap of making assumptions about the Killer and of going on talking into the silence. He assumes that the Killer thinks happiness is impossible. That he is a pessimist, a nihilist, an anarchist. That he had a reason for killing Dany. That he hates women or thinks the human race is rotten. Or kills out of kindness, to save people from suffering. Getting no reaction except the continual chuckle, Bérenger changes tack. Does the Killer hate mankind, believe the existence of the universe to be a mistake? Christ died on the cross for him and Bérenger offers to embrace, to comfort him. He offers understanding, but shows none.

> You deny love, you doubt charity, it doesn't enter into your calculations, and you think charity's a cheat, don't you, don't you?
> *(Chuckles from the Killer)*
> I'm not blaming you. I don't despise you for that. After all, it's a point of view, a possible point of view, but between ourselves, listen here: what do you get out of all this? What good does it do *you?* Kill people if you like, but in your mind . . . leave them alive in the flesh.

Uselessly he talks about the uselessness of killing, the trouble it causes the police. He offers to see that the Killer is let off and to introduce him to girls. Disturbed at still getting no reaction, he tries to win the Killer's sympathy by confessing that he, too, has accesses of doubt. But since everything is dust and ashes, crime is just vanity too. He even tries, not very convincingly, to laugh back at the chuckling criminal. But finally he has to face the reality that the Killer kills without reason and that there is no reason for asking him to stop. Bérenger tries to make a virtue out of this lack of reason, pleading with him just *because* there is no reason—to stop killing if only for a month. Or even forty-eight hours. When the Killer produces a knife Bérenger at first seems very aggressive. He produces his two pistols but his anger runs out and he finds that he cannot shoot. That there is nothing he can do.

# Rhinoceros

*Rhinoceros* has a very considerable pre-history which starts about 1940 with an entry Ionesco made in a diary. He was writing about the Nazis:

> The police are rhinoceroses. The magistrates are rhinoceroses. You are the only man among the rhinoceroses. The rhinoceroses ask themselves how the world can have been run by men. You ask yourself: is it true the world once was run by men?[1]

He goes on to say that the state, the nation, are depersonalizing abstractions. Humanity does not exist; there are only human beings. Society does not exist. For Ionesco, the state of the rhinoceroses is a fantasy; for the rhinoceroses the real individual is a fantasy.

Watching his antifascist friends go through the process of conversion to fascism was a deeply disturbing, if not traumatic, experience. It took them between three weeks and two months to become enmeshed in the system. Sometimes he could see the change in them without a word being spoken. A significant silence, a smile, a certain glint in the eye.

> I was talking to him. He was still a man. Suddenly under my eyes I saw his skin hardening and thickening fearfully. His gloves, his shoes, become hooves; his hands become paws. A horn grows on his forehead, he becomes fierce, he charges furiously. He no longer knows how to talk. He is becoming a rhinoceros. All of a sudden. I wish I could do the same. But me, I can't.[2]

There is another entry about 1940 which describes how a friend of Ionesco's, a member of a group which was resisting not physically but mentally the racist propaganda machine, went over to the enemy. One day he said that though they were monsters, they seemed to be right about one point, if only one, out of 10,000. All the same, to be absolutely objective. . . . When he was asked what the one point was he said "For instance, when they say that the Jews. . . ." He was caught up in the infernal machine. This was the first symptom.

Early in 1942, Ionesco was finding it very difficult to write at all. The whole western tradition seemed to be in danger of being wiped out, whether by a Nazi victory or a successful communist revolution. He noted in his diary how an English traveler who left France in April 1789 returned in October and said that he could no longer recognize the country. People had different expressions, they walked differently, talked differently, even the streets looked different. *There had been a mutation*, Ionesco comments, and it seemed to him that the same thing had happened now. The new men—Romanians, Germans, Russians and perhaps even the French—were a different race, a different genus. One he did not belong to.

Here clearly are the origins of *Rhinoceros*. But what is curious is that when he wrote the story *Rhinoceros*, which he published in 1957, he had completely forgotten his use of the word "rhinoceros" to describe the Nazis. It was only comparatively recently, when he rediscovered the old diary, that he saw the connection.

Undoubtedly the experience and the way he saw it influenced his reading of Kafka. The first book of his that Ionesco read was *Metamorphosis* and what struck him most forcibly of all was the statement it seemed to be making about guilt and the monster in each one of us that can rise to the surface and take over, just as it can in a whole community.

> Wars, uprisings, pogroms, collective frenzies and collective crimes, tyrannies and oppressions; these are just some aspects of the revelation of our monstrousness.[3]

When he wrote the Rhinoceros story he was still thinking of how the process of Nazification could metamorphose a community, but as he said in a 1961 article in *Arts*, the appeal of his individualistic hero to audiences in so many different countries made him wonder whether he had hit upon "a new plague of modern times, a strange disease that thrives in different forms, but is in principle the same. Automatic systematized thinking, the idolization of ideologies, screens the mind from reality, perverts our understanding and makes us blind. Ideologies too raise the barricades, dehumanize men and make it impossible for them to be *friends notwithstanding*; they get in the way of what we call coexistence, for a rhinoceros can only come to terms with one of his kind, a sectarian with a member of his particular sect."[4] In any case, in the resultant play, left wing totalitarianism and conformism are almost equally implicated. This was obvious to the Russians. Before staging the play in Moscow they asked Ionesco to revise the text in such a way that rhinoceritis would refer only to fascism. When he refused they abandoned their production plans.

Undoubtedly he did well to expand the rhinoceros metaphor into a story before making it into a play. It cannot have been easy to face the problems of staging an action in which the characters, one after another, turn into rhinoceroses. Even the first scene, a rhinoceros stampeding through a street, would not seem ideal for the theater, and by writing it up as a story Ionesco was able to develop the idea without worrying about dramatizing it.

Another technique, quite useful in the plays, which he seems to have taught himself from the stories is the technique of taking a key point in the plot for granted without ever having gone out of his way to plant it. Jean in *Rhinoceros*, like Edouard in *The Killer*, is an unlikely friend for Bérenger, but in both cases we accept the friendship because Ionesco makes no attempt to justify it. Bérenger himself is hardly the same character that he was in *The Killer*. In neither play is he characterized in the conventional sense, but in *Rhinoceros* he starts off with something of the lackadaisical disposition that was used for Edouard in *The Killer*. He also drinks too much. These points appear only in the play, not in the story, and the reason for them seems to be that Ionesco wants to make his character change during the action. Jean seems far more intelligently disciplined and capable of more imaginative effort than Bérenger, but he turns out to be an easy victim of rhinoceritis, while his friend reveals a strength of which there is no sign at all at the outset. He is the one character capable of holding out against it. Not that the strength of character Jean displays is intended to engage our sympathy. He is self-righteous, puritanical, overprecise and overfond of scientific explanations. As with the Logician, Ionesco satirizes him through the dryness of what he says.

The appearance of a rhinoceros in the town is dramatized in the only way it can be: through sound effects, reports of what has happened, and people's reactions. These reactions are stylized. Everybody says "Oh, a rhinoceros" and then "Well, of all things." Everybody except the Logician, whose first line is illogical: "Fear is an illogical thing. It must yield to reason." In the speculation about where the rhinoceros could come from, Bérenger is vague, Jean informed and precise. He also shows his irascibility. But often when Ionesco has a large group of characters he writes superfluous dialogue. (Other examples are the third act of *Amédée* and the offstage voices at the beginning of the third act of *The Killer*.) In this scene one of the functions of the low density dialogue is to space out the rhinoceros manifestations.

Some of the dialogue introduces themes that are already familiar from Ionesco's earlier work, as when Bérenger says he is drinking to get rid of the leaden feeling—a recurrent heaviness. Some of the comedy is reminiscent of Ionesco's earlier manner, as when the Logician proves syllogistically that a dog and Socrates are both cats. But in this first act there is no attempt to play up to any equivalent of the climacteric accelerando in the early plays or to the murder that closes Act One of *The Killer*. This is the first of the five plays based on stories which has no thriller element in it at all—nothing to do with policemen or corpses. And this first act is more purely a preparation for what is to follow. It closes fairly quietly with the ludicrous cortège of mourners for the cat which has been trampled to death by the rhinoceros. The people agree unanimously that they are not going to put up with the rhinoceros situation, while Bérenger decides to drink instead of keeping the promise he made Jean to cultivate his mind by going to the museum.

The office in which the first scene of Act Two is set provides a more satisfactory microcosm than the café of Act One for representing the social reaction to the rhinoceros incidents. It does not matter to Ionesco whether it is a government office or the office of a large publishing concern—perhaps publishing law books. Botard, a sixty-year-old ex-schoolmaster, refuses to believe in the rhinoceroses; Dudard, a qualified lawyer of thirty-five, argues with him on the basis of what he has read in the papers and what other people have said, while Papillon, the head of the department, protests against their wasting office time on the conversation. One of the employees, Boeuf, has failed to put in an appearance today, and halfway through the scene his wife rushes in, panting, to say that she has been chased by a rhinoceros which is now trying to climb the staircase. Ionesco makes the presence of the rhinoceros seem like an immediate reality when the staircase collapses. We hear the anguished trumpeting and an enormous crash. The stage is filled with clouds of dust. When they clear we see that the staircase landing is hanging in space. Botard still tries to insist that the rhinoceros is an illusion until they all see it outside going round and round trumpeting as if in pain.

When Mme. Boeuf recognizes it as her husband, Papillon announces that he is sacked, only to be threatened by Botard with union action. Daisy, a blond equivalent of Dany, telephones the fire brigade to come to their rescue but Mme. Boeuf is so impatient to join her husband she will not wait for ladders to be brought. She jumps out of the window and he gallops off with

her on his back. We realize we have witnessed the first
case of a human opting for mutation.

The difficulty Daisy has in getting the firemen to
come helps to establish the number of other incidents
there have been all over the town. Seven rhinoceroses
had been reported in the morning; now the number is
up to seventeen. Botard, who insistently politicizes
everything, hints darkly at a conspiracy. What is more,
he knows the names of the traitors responsible.

Throughout this scene, Ionesco is very clever in his
realization of offstage events. In the second scene of
Act Two, which is concentrated on an individual mutation, that of Jean, the technical problems are different.
Jean cannot change physically in front of us, so from
the moment Bérenger tells him that he has got a bump
on his forehead Ionesco has him keep going into the
bathroom to check his appearance in the mirror. This
enables the actor to adjust his make-up each time. His
skin turns progressively greener, the bump is gradually
enlarged, growing almost into a horn, and Ionesco
neatly sidesteps the problem of showing him when the
transformation is complete by having Bérenger shut
him in the bathroom, at the cost of having his coat
pierced as a rhinoceros horn penetrates through the
door.

All this has very little to do with language, but in the
next scene Ionesco uses dialogue effectively and very
economically to explore the conformism. Jean is ill in
bed, coughing hoarsely and he is bad-tempered from the
outset; when Bérenger well-meaningly urges him to see
a doctor, he says he has confidence only in vets. He gets
more and more angry, more like a pacing beast in a
cage. He makes "brrr" noises and he starts puffing.
The most difficult part of the scene to write must have
been the sequence in which we see his mind starting to

work like an animal's. He argues with Bérenger about the superiority of humanity. He is sick of moral standards, he says.

> JEAN: Nature has its own laws. Morality's against nature.
> BERENGER: Are you suggesting we replace our moral laws by the law of the jungle?
> JEAN: It would suit me, suit me fine.
> BERENGER: You say that. But deep down, no one . . .
> JEAN: We've got to build our life on new foundations. We must get back to primeval integrity.

When Bérenger cites the arguments that animals do not share the values which have evolved from centuries of civilization, Jean retorts that we will be better off as soon as we have demolished them. Humanism is sentimental. Though perfectly valid without knowledge of the play's antifascist origins, these conversations take on a different complexion in the light of it.

The same applies to the end of the scene which is theatrically effective on whatever level it is taken, but after *Présent passé passé présent* it is impossible not to see it as a quasi-allegorical re-creation of the incredulous frustration that ordinary, kindly citizens must have encountered in the thirties if they appealed to the civic authorities for help against the fascists. In the room opposite Jean's is an Old Man who was talkative earlier but becomes uncooperative when Bérenger says he has seen a rhinoceros in the house. Frightened, wanting to call the police, Bérenger rushes to the porter's lodge, only to find a rhinoceros head appears there. When he runs back past the Old Man's apartment, the door opens to reveal two rhinoceros heads. He tries to climb out of the window but retreats when he sees an army of rhinoceroses surging up the avenue. Meanwhile, the rhinoceros that was Jean has been battering against the bathroom door, which is just about to give in as the act ends.

In the final act Bérenger's fear of the rhinoceroses is eclipsed by his fear of the desire he now feels to become one. Lying in bed and coughing, as Jean had at the beginning of the previous scene, Bérenger is nervous that a bump will soon appear on his forehead. By making Dudard visit him, Ionesco is able to bring us up to date on affairs at the office. Papillon has turned into a rhinoceros, and when they look out of the window to see a boater impaled on a passing horn, we know that the Logician too has been transformed.

Dudard remains on stage for quite a while, both before and after the arrival of Daisy. These twenty minutes or so represent the last period of his life as a human being: at the end he will run out to join the animals. But what Ionesco shows us of his transformation is totally different from what we saw of Jean's. This scene has much more in common with Ionesco's description in his diary of how his friend showed that he was about to leap on to the broad back of the Nazi juggernaut when he said that they seemed to be right about one point, if only one out of 10,000. Ionesco may have forgotten this when he was writing the scene but certainly it forms the unconscious background. When Dudard says that it is essential to a scientific mentality to keep an open mind towards the rhinoceroses, to be impartial, if not favorably disposed, Bérenger comments that Dudard soon will be siding with them. The next step is for him to be willing to entertain the possibility that there is nothing abnormal in a man's turning into a rhinoceros. When they see the rhinoceros with the boater, he argues that, as a thinker, the Logician must have weighed the pros and cons before deciding, and when Daisy arrives with the news that Botard (who had been very acid about Papillon's becoming a rhinoceros) has become one himself, Dudard calls it "a case of community spirit triumphing over his anarchic impulses." Soon, like Jean, he is doubting whether man is superior to the rhinoceroses.

> DUDARD: I feel certain scruples! I feel it's my duty to stick by my employers and my friends, through thick and thin.
>
> BERENGER: It's not as if you were married to them.
>
> DUDARD: I've renounced marriage. I prefer the great universal family to the little domestic one.
>
> DAISY (*softly*): We shall miss you a lot, Dudard, but we can't do anything about it.
>
> DUDARD: It's my duty to stick by them; I have to do my duty.
>
> BERENGER: No, you're wrong, your duty is to . . . you don't see where your real duty lies . . . your duty is to oppose them, with a firm, clear mind.
>
> DUDARD: I shall keep my mind clear. (*He starts to move round the stage in circles*) As clear as ever it was. But if you're going to criticize, it's better to do so from the inside.

After he has gone, Bérenger feels guilty, both on his own account for not having saved Jean, and on Daisy's: if she had been gentler in rejecting the pass Papillon made at her, perhaps he would have remained human. The scene is developed to give us the impression of two lonely humans surrounded by rhinoceroses. More and more noises of trampling and trumpeting are heard outside. The telephone rings and trumpetings are heard at the other end. When they switch the radio on (or in Orson Welles's production, the television) they find that it has been taken over by rhinoceroses. At first the isolation they share makes them feel love for each other but soon Daisy is weakening.

> DAISY: I feel a bit ashamed of what you call love
> —this morbid feeling, this male weakness. And
> female too. It just doesn't compare with the
> ardour and the tremendous energy emanating
> from all these creatures around us.
> BERENGER: Energy! You want some energy, do
> you? I can let you have some energy! (*He slaps
> her face.*)

Neither his immediate contrition nor his realization that in a few minutes they have gone through twenty-five years of married life can reverse the rapid ebb of their feeling for each other. Soon she is saying the rhinoceroses are beautiful and godlike, then she runs out on him to join them. Ionesco has compared Bérenger's isolation among the proliferating rhinoceroses with the New Tenant's final isolation among the furniture. The closing monologue is more reminiscent of Bérenger's final confrontation with the Killer. Here, as there, his final faith in humanity is being put to a severe test. Again, within minutes, he has started to weaken. He wishes he could grow a horn; a forehead without one has come to seem ugly. Starting to hate his white hairy body he tries to imitate the trumpeting he hears outside. But it is too late for him to change, even if he feels monstrous in his human form, and with a sudden defiance, the monologue ends on a upbeat. If necessary he will take on the whole lot of them. He will not capitulate.

In *Notes and Counter Notes*, Ionesco has said that though *Rhinoceros* is a farce, it is above all a tragedy. Which mood predominates depends partly on how the play is directed.

The odd thing is that when you don't use any props the play becomes blacker, more tragic; when you do use use them, it's comic, people laugh.[5]

In the Düsseldorf production it was primarily tragic, in Jean-Louis Barrault's it was comic. Both interpretations are valid; Ionesco prefers the comic.

# Frenzy for Two

*Frenzy for Two . . . and the Same to You* is much shorter and much less substantial than *Rhinoceros*, but has certain themes in common with it. The violence which is chiefly an undertone in *Rhinoceros* is a background at the beginning of *Frenzy for Two* and penetrates more into the foreground as the action progresses, as in *The Chairs* and *The New Tenant*, where by the end of the play the furniture becomes more important than the actors. After shooting and sounds of gunfire we have a bullet which breaks the windowpane. Then a hand grenade is thrown in through the window and the man throws it out again only to be blamed by the woman when it explodes. A statue falls through a hole in the ceiling, then another missile comes through the wall to fall on the floor. Then the mirror is broken as rubble falls from the ceiling. Ionesco asks for the ceiling to disappear altogether by the end of the play. The climax of proliferation comes when headless bodies, and bodiless heads are seen hanging down from the floor above, where a guillotine, they say, has been installed.

So the surface is very different from that of *Rhinoceros*, but basically Ionesco is concerned with the correspondence between private aggression and warfare, personal violence and public violence. Unlike the couples in all his other plays, the man and the woman are not married. She left her husband for him seventeen years ago and he left his wife for her, but now they irritate each other and she blames him—as he blames her—for her abandonment of her family. Both of them talk resentfully of what their lives might have been but for the other: at one point he tries to leave her, but hand grenades are being thrown. She blames him for living in this no man's land between the two sections. Later she almost goads him into going without her to hide in the cellar, but it is cold and raining.

The action starts with an absurd argument: she is stubbornly maintaining that there is no difference between a snail and a tortoise. She proves it with a pseudosyllogism: both have shells, sometimes retreat into them, both are slimy with short bodies and both move slowly. Under pressure she adjusts her position— a snail only has a horn when it is shown, while a tortoise is "a snail that doesn't." Starting the play with these creatures which have shells is significant—there is nowhere where the humans can draw away from the violence, though they try to barricade the shutters with mattresses, and when the play ends they are blocking all the windows and doors, hoping to seal themselves off. But even in the midst of doing this they are quarreling and slapping each other.

# A Stroll in the Air

In January 1962, when Ionesco wrote the short story *Le piéton de l'air*, he had not written a play since *Rhinoceros* in 1958. (*Frenzy for Two* was written in November 1962, after the play bearing the English title *A Stroll in the Air* had been finished the previous summer. The beginning of the story alludes specifically to the writer's abandonment of the theater some years earlier in a state of resentment provoked by the malevolence of certain of his critics and the stubborn blindness of the rest.

The story is the longest in *The Colonel's Photograph* and, of the five that he made into plays, it is the least theatrical. This, he said, is what made the prospect of dramatizing it so tempting.

> Even the opposite of theater can become theater. It was a challenge . . . How could I make a play out of *The Stroller*, out of a man flying off and passers-by telling stories, rather than out of simple, present conflicts? That was what tempted me.[1]

115

But whereas in *Rhinoceros* he succeeded in making something thoroughly theatrical out of unpromising material, on *A Stroll in the Air* he did not.

His starting point for both the story and the play was his recurring dream about flying. Combined with this at an early stage of the conception was his vision of the horrors of life under totalitarianism. This is what Bérenger sees when he is flying.

> Quite simply, what's going on in half the world, and what the other half, out of blindness, indifference, or obstinacy, doesn't want to see: dozens of millions of people humiliated; terror enthroned, tyranny, power gone mad, the regular little everyday apocalypse, men licking idols' arses, and other things that are catastrophically amusing.[2]

Just as the Bérenger of *Rhinoceros* was a different character from the Bérenger in *The Killer*, here he is different again and quite unlike the King Bérenger I of *Exit the King*. Of all four Bérengers, this one is closest to Ionesco himself, and much of what he says in the interviews he gives the Journalist more or less corresponds to Ionesco's own feelings. Bérenger says that he had always known he had no reason to write, that he is a nihilist with nothing to say and cannot go on turning out plays. That literature, however cruel it becomes, can only give a dim picture of the cruelty of life. That anything would be tolerable if only we were immortal, but that he is paralyzed by the knowledge he will die.

If we did not know he had had the story to use as a scenario, it would be tempting to conjecture that Ionesco had written this uninspired and undramatic opening in the hope that he would find out from it how to go on. The interview has been preceded by an open-air sequence in which two English Ladies tell each other that they are English, exchanging redundant information rather in the manner of the English characters in *The Bald Soprano*, while two married couples, each with a child, exchange polite remarks. So neither of the first two sequences creates any tension.

The next section dramatizes the dream described in the short story by the narrator's wife. Josephine appears with the Doctor-Uncle and the Undertaker's Man. Her father, who died in the war, has come back to life. The Undertaker, who talks as if the corpse had not yet been buried, threatens legal action. Through this dialogue a plane has been heard approaching. Now it drops a bomb on Bérenger's cottage, which is left as a pile of smoking ruins. All the English characters reappear, together with John Bull, but, like Josephine and her daughter, Marthe, they do not talk about the bomb. Apart from the little boy, who says he wants to be a pilot when he grows up so that he can drop bombs on people's houses, the only one to refer to it is Bérenger, who explains that it was a German bomber left over from the last war. (We are not told how much time is meant to have gone by since the war ended.)

The little girl wants to be a prima donna when she grows up and after she has trilled like a mechanical nightingale, and after John Bull, to illustrate how differently his grandfather used to sing the same song, has produced exactly the same trill, her wig is pulled off to reveal that she is bald. Altogether, Ionesco seems to be laboring here to produce effects that are scarcely worth producing. That the bombing is taken so much for granted does produce a considerable effect but it is followed by too much padding, as in the conversation about buying a new handbag for Josephine.

The walk they take does offer the possibility of imaginative visual effects. The English characters cross the stage singly or in pairs while a curtain or screen moves in the same direction and the Bérenger family seems to be walking in the opposite direction. A train is heard in the distance and we see the miniature engine chugging along with tiny red passenger cars. The dialogue gives us a montage of fragments from the conversations of the promenaders, mostly reflecting familiar preoccupations, the uselessness of trying to change one's life, the uselessness of regretting the past, the way children of today play with rockets rather than dolls. The sound of melodious singing makes Bérenger say that it is sirens' voices from the ships. A turreted palace comes into view and fields with motionless, grazing cows. As the screen keeps moving, we see a little Eiffel Tower, a red balloon floating away, a blue lake and a waterfall, the terminus of a telpher railway, and a little rocket vanishing in a shower of sparks, then woods again and trees in blossom. At least the stage directions ask for all this. Meanwhile the dialogue is undramatic and generalizing. The First Lady talks about the need to get used to dying (a theme to be developed in *Exit the King*) and the Journalist divides people into two categories: the contemplative man who wants to be in harmony with the world, and the man of action who wants to bring the world into harmony with himself. Which is the right solution, he asks. All this dialogue is rather like what Chekhov might have written if he had not been able to write.

The play becomes more like a Ionesco play when the Visitor from the antiworld appears, with white side-whiskers and old-fashioned clothes. His pipe is upside down in his mouth and the smoke from it goes downwards. He passes very close to the Bérengers without seeming to see them, while Josephine does not see him (though Bérenger and Marthe do). When he vanishes Bérenger explains that he is not a creature of this world. He has gone back to the antiworld through a wall which is invisible but opaque. Bérenger admits there is no proof that the antiworld exists.

> But when you think about it, you can find it in your own thoughts. The evidence is in your mind. There's not just one antiworld. There are several universes, and they're all interlocking.

This is the kind of assumption which is recurrent in Ionesco's thinking: that the desire to believe in something implies its existence in reality. The psychological need for religion means that God probably exists; since none of us want to die we must have been *intended* to be immortal.

Bérenger goes on to explain that there is an unknown quantity of universes, all interlinking and interlocking without touching each other, all coexisting in the same space. One of the Englishwomen interrupts the conversation with what she calls visual proof. In Ireland and in Scotland she has seen in mirrors the outline of a landscape which is not ours. Another English Lady says that as soon as a dead body is put into a coffin it vanishes.

> BERENGER: Those who leave us settle down so to speak, for good in the antiworld, and they have antiheads . . .
> 2nd WOMAN: They have antiheads.
> JOHN BULL: Antiheads, antilimbs, anticlothes, antifeelings and antihearts.

According to Bérenger, there is proof in our language that the negative of our universe exists. A phrase like "the world turned upside down" originated from the antiworld. A great deal of dialogue has already been devoted to the explaining of this mumbo-jumbo metaphysics, an exposition that has little connection with

anything that went before except the announcement of
the resurrection of Josephine's father, which had already
introduced the notion of the reversibility of the mortality process. But from now on, Ionesco produces a series
of stage conjuring tricks to illustrate the argument in
the dialogue. As they go on walking, a little pink column
covered with flowers rises out of the ground. It has
emerged from the void, Bérenger explains, describing
the void as a kind of box.

> Every world and everything in these worlds goes
> into it and comes out of it, and yet it's very tiny,
> tinier than the tiniest cavity, tinier than the tiniest
> hollow in dice, tinier than tininess itself, because
> it has no dimension at all. You see, ruins like this,
> a relic of palaces that have ceased to exist, will be
> entirely swept away, of course, but perhaps, per-
> haps—and that's where there's a glimmer of hope
> —when they've passed through the void, they'll all
> be reconstructed and restored on the other side;
> inside out, naturally, as it's on the other side.
> Perhaps the rebuilding has already started; the
> stones and the ruins that disappear are being put
> together again out there. And the same with every-
> thing. And everything's aware of this, and that's
> what explains the happiness all about us, this
> feeling of victory, the beauty of the day.

When a tree vanishes, it has been sucked into the void.
The tree and the column keep appearing and disappearing, as does the Visitor from the antiworld, who sometimes makes a partial reappearance—his leg and his
pipe, or his body without his head. Some of Bérenger's
explanations are made in asides, representing unspoken
thoughts which his attentive wife manages to hear.
This corresponds to a passage in the short story where
she manages to read his thoughts, and like the passage

in the story *A Victim of Duty* where the Detective penetrates into Choubert's unspoken thoughts, it cannot possibly be so effective when dramatized.

Richard Coe sees a connection between Bérenger's metaphysics and Ionesco's interest in Zen Buddhism.

> For, according to the teachings of Zen, all that has a finite and positive existence is the obstacle which prevents man's reunion with the timeless, dimensionless not-being of God. Consequently, the absurdity, the unmeaning of all that exists in Ionesco's original hypothesis is the necessary corollary of any ultimate intuition of the totality which is God. God *is* what "all-that-exists" is *not*. And so the absurdity and significance of all existing phenomena now offer the mystic's surest path to the haven of nirvana—which, after all, is itself a néant; a "positive zero" or, in the special language of Zen, a "plenum Void."[3]

Coe has said that with his play Ionesco was moving away from 'Pataphysics and he agrees that it was becoming less important for him at this time. But the argument that is woven into both the dialogue and the action is very reminiscent of Jarry and his undetectable shifts from straightforward expositions of serious scientific experiments* to sheer nonsense. This mixture of

* Such as C. V. Boys's experiments with soap bubbles which were meant to prove that water had an elastic skin, and Lord Kelvin's experiments with the measuring rod, the watch, the tuning fork, the luminiferous ether, the rotating flywheel and linked gyrostats. The appeal of 'Pataphysics seems to lie largely in its combination of irreverence and irresponsibility with the possibility of stumbling on ideas which have serious implications but can be treated noncommittally. In his Introduction to the Methuen (London) edition of *Jarry's Selected Works*, Roger Shattuck has compared the anagogical interpretations of medieval commentators with the 'Pataphysicians systematic toying with the arrangement of things and their significance until we see the improbable hypothesis as real (p. 18).

science and nonsense is characteristic of Jarry's "neo-scientific novel" *The Exploits and Opinions of Dr Faustroll, 'Pataphysician.* It defines 'Pataphysics as:

> the science of that which is superinduced upon metaphysics, whether within or beyond the latter's limitations, extending as far beyond metaphysics as the latter extends beyond physics . . . 'Pataphysics will examine the laws governing excep-tions, and will explain the universe supplementary to this one; or, less ambitiously, will describe a universe which can be—and perhaps should be—envisaged in the place of the traditional one, since the laws that are supposed to have been discovered in the traditional universe are also correlations of exceptions, albeit more frequent ones, but in any case accidental data which, reduced to the status of unexceptional exceptions, possess no longer even the virtue of originality.[4]

*A Stroll in the Air* seems to have been influenced by Book 8 of *Dr. Faustroll,* which starts with a telepathic letter to Lord Kelvin saying that Dr. Faustroll is not dead but elsewhere than on the earth. He says that eternity appears to him in the image of an immobile ether which he dubs ethernity. The final chapter has the title "Concerning the Surface of God," and it starts with the contention that God has no dimensions but that it is permissible, for the sake of clarity, to endow him with any number of them if they vanish on both sides of our identities. The chapter leads to the conclusion that God is the tangential point between zero and infinity.

Ionesco may also have been influenced by Jarry's deadpan essay "How to Construct a Time Machine," which describes space as the locus of bodies just as time is the locus of events. It refers to the four-dimensional space implied by the intersection of several three-dimensional spaces and to:

> Riemannian spaces, which, being spheres, are closed, since the circle is a geodesic line on the sphere of the same radius.[5]

It goes on to say that the present is extended in three directions. If one transfers oneself to any point in the past or future, this point will be the present and extended in three directions as long as one occupies it. It is not hard to explain the appeal of this idea to Ionesco or to anyone who is fixated on the notion of immortality and the irreversibility of time. Jarry, in both his fiction and his nonfiction—which are not in fact always so very different from each other—was making a valid point by blurring the distinction between 'Pataphysics and the findings of contemporary physicists. It can be argued that he anticipates Heisenberg, however fortuitously. But there are boring sequences in Jarry just as there are in A Stroll in the Air, which only begins to come into its own as a play when the flying starts.

This happens when a big silver bridge appears on the screen, joining two sides of a gorge over an abyss. The beauty of it gives Bérenger a feeling of lightness and airiness. Gaily jumping up and down he says how miserable he is when he thinks of the years going by like sacks we send back empty, and of how we are all going to leave one another. He is making winglike gestures with his arms and soon the uncontrollable feeling of gaiety has lifted his feet a few inches off the ground. Watching him, the English characters are slightly disturbed, especially when the instinct to fly proves to be infectious. First the children and then the adults start hopping about in imitation of him. This sequence is followed rather oddly by a passage in which all the dialogue is sung.

Soon Bérenger is able, quite effortlessly, to leap much higher into the air—three feet, six feet. A man has a crying need to fly, he says. It is as necessary and as natural as breathing and he has found the way to do it again. Everybody knows how to fly but forgets. We rise above our instincts when we fly above them. All you need is confidence. You come down when you lose confidence.

When he begins to explain the tricks of flying to Marthe, a one-wheeled circus bicycle is thrown on from the wings and simultaneously tiers of seats appear. The other characters become a circus audience as Bérenger demonstrates, cycling up into the air on the bicycle while Marthe cycles below. (It is possible that this episode was partly inspired by Jarry's "The Passion Considered as an Uphill Bicycle Race," with its irreverent description of Jesus riding flat on his back on his cross-frame machine in order to reduce the air resistance.)

Next Bérenger climbs into an imaginary tree, jerking himself higher and higher, but Marthe and the little English boy, who both try to follow him, cannot get off the ground. Then Bérenger hits the ground a little too hard with his feet and flies right away. The other characters by their dialogue and the movement of their heads describe the orbit of his course, which is represented by a glowing ball appearing and disappearing, moving with increasing speed. He flies higher and higher and after he vanishes the stage darkens with blood-red glimmering lights and loud rumbles of thunder or bombardment.

Isolated by a spotlight, Josephine complains of her terror at being left alone, as she so often is. The

Journalist and the Second Englishman are seen transformed (possibly by masks representing their own faces) into dream figures. In friendly tones they talk about friendship as being a mere cover for loathing. Josephine continues her lament about her solitude, which becomes partly a lament for the loss of her childhood, the comfort of having parents to look after her. Now John Bull and the little boy reappear, also transformed into dream figures, with John Bull chasing the boy to vent his aggressiveness on him.

Also transformed, several of the choric characters commiserate with Josephine, and the climax of this sequence comes when a gigantic crimson Judge appears, seven to ten feet tall, with a solid doll's head, terrifying and funny at the same time. It is Josephine who is on trial, and though Marthe tells her it is a nightmare, she is unable to wake up from it. In anguish she protests her innocence—how she has always been a dutiful wife. Finally the vision fades but John Bull returns with a machine gun to shoot the two children. The Doctor-Uncle, called in to confirm that they are defunct, assures Josephine that he does not accept what has been happening—he is just resigned to it.

> Besides, it's better this way. In any case it was bound to happen. It's all over much quicker this way. It's better sooner than later, much better to be thirty years early than two seconds too late.

Now the Great White Man appears, accompanied by a hangman in white with a gibbet. He tries to persuade Josephine not to put off dying until later:

> You know very well you can't escape. You know very well that everyone goes the same way. You don't gain anything really, only a little time.

He frightens her but fails to persuade her and when he disappears, the light becomes first blood-red again, then grey, and Bérenger's despairing voice is heard, wishing that it were only a dream. Now he is spinning slowly round, the choric characters tell us, like a top which is running down. When he reappears to the sound of derisively triumphant dance music, he is in a deep depression. The English belittle his achievement, at first saying that instead of flying he was walking on an invisible arch, then that there is nothing interesting or extraordinary about it.

Asked what he saw, he replies very disappointingly in images that do not match up to the effectiveness of the nightmare sequence we have been watching in his absence. It is often problematic for Ionesco to co-ordinate the descriptions in his dialogue with the visual images he invents. Bérenger speaks of seeing men with the heads of geese, men licking monkeys' behinds and drinking the sows' piss, columns of headless men crossing enormous plains, giant grasshoppers, fallen angels, and archangels gone astray. He talks of continents of paradise all in flames, the blessed being burned alive, knives, graves, mountains caving in, oceans of blood. The Journalist says he hasn't seen any of it but simply read it in the Apocalypse, and the First Man says that none of this can compare with Dante. As at the end of *Improvisation*, Ionesco is amusingly self-critical, and here he shows how Bérenger loses his audience as he goes on talking about reaching the ridge of the invisible roof where time and space come together. The parents must take their children home to bed, the Journalist invites John Bull to the pub, and Bérenger is unable to make them listen to his Cassandra cries of bottomless pits opening over the plains, millions of disappearing universes, infinite wastes of fire and ice, and tremendous curtains of flames.

But, as in *Improvisation*, the implied self-criticism is justified. The imagery is not set organically in a dramatic context to give it the force it needs, and the end is weak. When Josephine and Marthe ask him to fly them away beyond the other side of hell he says he cannot because there is nothing there. They go out, hoping it will all come right in the end, amid spluttering firecrackers of what Bérenger explains is a kind of English Fourteenth of July.*

* A French national holiday.

# Exit the King

Unlike the three other Bérenger plays, *Exit the King* made its first appearance not as a short story but as the scenario for a ballet, with a story far more romantic than it became in the play. The palace is crumbling—pieces of wall are being propped up by the dancers, the King, the Queen, and the rest. The strange Princess with whom the senile King tries to dance turns out to be death, but in dying he regains the vigor and the good looks he had as a young man.

The purpose of the play is very different. Ionesco has described it to Claude Bonnefoy as "an attempt at an apprenticeship in dying."[1]

> *Exit the King* was written in twenty days. I wrote first of all for ten days. I had just been ill and I'd been very scared. Then, after these ten days, I had a relapse and was ill for another fortnight. At the end of the fortnight, I started work again. I finished the play in the next ten days. Only I realized, on rereading it, and again when I saw the

play on the stage, that the first half had a rhythm
that was no longer the same in the second half.[2]

In the Paris production the play seemed ready to end
when it was only half over, but when Robert Postec
directed it in Brussels he emphasized the change of
rhythm instead of camouflaging it. He took Bérenger's
lines "And if I decided not to die" as the turning point.
By flooding the darkening stage with fresh light and
making the characters who had been clustering round
the throne go back to their original positions, he created
the feeling that the dying King really might be able to
cling on to life.[3] For Ionesco, the fact of mortality has
always been what he hates most about the human
condition. He describes in his *Fragments of a Journal*
how at the age of four or five he realized he was becoming older, that he would die. When he was seven or
eight he frightened himself with the realization that
his mother would die before he would. Living in the
country, away from her, he felt as though he were outside time, in a paradisal state; but when he was eleven
or twelve he was stricken with the sense of an ending.
He still cannot understand how he can become passion-
ate or even preoccupied with economic, social or
political problems when he knows (1) that we are going
to die (2) that revolution does not save us from life
or death (3) that he cannot imagine a finite or infinite
universe. Death, he says, is the goal of existence. None
of Ionesco's characters ever voices his own basic preoccupation more clearly than King Bérenger I when he
asks "Why was I born if it wasn't for ever?"

As so often in Ionesco, the weather prevailing in the
individual world penetrates to the atmosphere outside.
It is not just the King that is crumbling. It is the whole
cosmos. The general feeling of ultimate dereliction re-

sembles that of Beckett's *Endgame*: the cow is running out of milk and the sun was late in rising, though the Guard heard the King ordering it to come out. As King, Bérenger is responsible for the general decay:

> MARGUERITE: His palace is crumbling. His fields lie fallow. His mountains are sinking. The sea has broken the dykes and flooded the country. He's let it all go to rack and ruin . . . Instead of conserving the soil, he's let acre upon acre plunge into the bowels of the earth. . . . Not to mention all those disastrous wars. While his drunken soldiers were sleeping it off, at night or after a lavish lunch in barracks, our neighbors were pushing back our frontier posts. Our national boundaries were shrinking. His soldiers didn't want to fight . . . The victorious armies called them cowards and deserters, and they were shot. You can see the result; towns razed to the ground, burnt-out swimming pools, abandoned bistros. The young are leaving their homeland in hordes. At the start of his reign there were nine thousand million inhabitants . . . And now about a thousand people left. Less. Even now, while I'm talking, they're passing away.
>
> MARIE: There are forty-five young people, too.
>
> MARGUERITE: No one else wants *them*. *We* didn't want them either; we were forced to take them back. Anyway, they're ageing fast. Repatriated at twenty-five, two days later and they're over eighty.

The two Queens, Marguerite and Marie, Bérenger's first and second wives, are the counterparts to the Queen and the Princess of the ballet. Marguerite, ageing and realistic, is often harsh in her criticisms, and if she helps Bérenger towards an acceptance of the death that is waiting for him, she does it none too gently. Marie, besides being young and beautiful, is very gentle and loving, often almost motherly towards the old man, a good comforter but too romantic to help him to come to terms with the harshness of reality and death.

While King Bérenger is the first male in Ionesco to have the female role in his life divided between two women, several of the other characters combine a number of roles as the Architect did in *The Killer*. The Doctor is also surgeon, executioner, bacteriologist, and astrologer. Juliette, the nurse, is also the domestic help. The Guard also performs the function of major domo, announcing the characters as they enter, and, acting as a chorus, commenting directly to the audience.

As in *The Chairs* the preoccupations with the themes of life and age, deterioration and death, worldly achievement and nothingness are pursued without any attachment to a social or political context. Halberds coexist anachronistically with radiators and Bérenger is apparently over 500 years old. According to Marguerite, he married two hundred and eighty-three years ago and has been reigning for two hundred and seventy-seven years and three months. But to him it seems like a matter of minutes and he wants to go back to being a baby. When the Doctor confirms that he is dying, his response is that he knows he will die—in forty or fifty or three hundred years. When he has time.

Two of the important sources of the mood and imagery of the play seem to be legend and Shakespearean tragedy. A crumbling castle, the references to astrology, and a great deal of the King's behavior are reminiscent of nursery stories, as are the description of how the ministers have gone away on holiday, and the way that cobwebs keep reappearing in the royal bedroom as soon as Juliette has brushed them away. When Bérenger keeps falling over and stumbling to his feet, the stage direction asks that the scene should be played like a tragic Punch and Judy show. When he gives orders to nature, he sounds like King Canute, but much of the cosmic imagery is reminiscent of Shakespearean tragedies like *Macbeth* and *Julius Caesar,* in which the disorder in the body politic is accompanied by unnatural cosmic manifestations. In Ionesco these apocalyptic symptoms become comic. The Doctor reports that since Mars and Saturn collided, the sun has lost between fifty and seventy-five per cent of its strength. Yesterday evening it was spring but now it is November. Cows are calving twice a day in other countries but here the trees are sighing and dying. The earth is quaking more than usual, the lightning has stuck in the sky, the clouds are raining frogs and the thunder is mumbling. But whereas Shakespeare takes the correspondence between the microcosm and the macrocosm, the King's person and the social body, for granted, here the theme is made explicit:

> I am the dying agony of them all. My death is manifold. So many worlds will flicker out in me.

This is developed in the second half of the action until he becomes an embodiment of the whole of human civilization. The Guard's choric commentary makes claims on his behalf, identifying him not only with Prometheus but with the inventor of the airplane.

> It was he who invented gunpowder and stole fire from the gods. He nearly blew the whole place up. But he caught the pieces and tied them together again with string. I helped him, but it wasn't so easy. *He* wasn't so easy either. He was the one who fitted up the first forges on earth. He discovered the way to make steel. He used

to work eighteen hours a day. And he made us work even harder. He was our chief engineer. As an engineer he made the first balloon, and then the Zeppelin. And, finally, with his own hands, he built the first airplane. At the start it wasn't a success. The first test pilots, Icarus and the rest, all fell into the sea. Till eventually he piloted the plane himself. I was his mechanic. Long before that, when he was only a little prince, he'd invented the wheelbarrow. I used to play with him. Then rails and railways and automobiles. He drew up the plans for the Eiffel Tower, not to mention his designs for the sickle and the plough, the harvesters and the tractors.

KING: Tractors? Good Heavens, yes! I'd forgotten.

GUARD: He extinguished volcanoes and caused new ones to erupt. He built Rome, New York, Moscow and Geneva. He *founded* Paris. He created revolutions, counterrevolution, religion, reform, and counterreform.

He goes on to tell us he wrote Shakespeare's plays, invented the telephone and the telegraph. Marie says he also created the sun on the day he was born. But Ionesco is not content to leave these cosmic claims in verbal form. The cosmos of the play is the set, and we see the crack in the wall widening and other new cracks appearing as the frantic beating of the King's heart, audible all over the auditorium, shakes the palace. The crack on the wall has already been interpreted—rather like the writing on the wall of Nebuchadnezzar's palace—as a sign that there is no hope.

The theme of the individual's adjustment to the reality of his own death is held firmly in the center of all this elaboration. In his first speech, Bérenger is in a state of complete ignorance about his own condition. He has got a headache and his legs are a bit stiff but he thinks he is still sufficiently in command of things to give orders to the clouds. His self-absorption is played off against a joking awareness of the condition the country is in and a vague desire to set things right. Affectionately Marie convinces him that he is limping, and that his leg hurts but it is in vain that she tries to stop Marguerite from telling him the truth.

> MARGUERITE: You're going to die in an hour and a half, you're going to die at the end of the show.
>
> KING: What did you say, my dear? That's not funny.
>
> MARGUERITE: You're going to die at the end of the show.
>
> MARIE: Oh God!
>
> DOCTOR: Yes, Sire, you are going to die. You will not take breakfast tomorrow morning. Nor will you dine tonight.

Bérenger's first reaction is that no one could have given such orders without his consent. He tries to move about and when he finds that he cannot, he says it is because he was not mentally prepared. When Marguerite and the Doctor advise him to abdicate voluntarily he orders the Guard to arrest them but the Guard does not move. The army, says the Doctor, is paralyzed and Marguerite tells the King that it is his own orders which have paralyzed the man, who readily obeys orders from Marguerite and the Doctor but not from Bérenger. Even Marie, who tries to please him by obeying his orders, finds that she cannot. He has been condemned, Marguerite says, and he should have trained himself by thinking about death for a few minutes each day, gradually stepping up the time. He says he will never resign himself to dying, though he has caused the deaths of many other people. When he refuses an injection, he says he knows what they mean because he has had them given to other people before. (The Nazis used injections for killing.) He has also ordered the executions of his rivals, including Marguerite's parents and his own relations. And now he prays for the death of every other living creature, providing he can live for ever. But Ionesco does not allow this unscrupulousness in Bérenger to make him more than momentarily unsympathetic.

Ionesco has said that he himself has never quite succeeded in getting used to existence, that he goes through life perpetually astonished at everything that happens to him. Above all at the fact of aging: he still sometimes feels surprised at no longer being a twelve-year-old. From being incredulous and delighted at the sensation of being alive, he went to extremes of anguish and fear of being devoured by "the darkness of nothingness" (*les ténèbres du Néant*).[5]

The King similarly oscillates between a delighted apprehension of reality and moments of realization that death is inevitable. He makes an effort to break beyond the frontiers of his solipsism by questioning Juliette about her life. When she describes it as a bad life, his answer is that "bad life" is a contradiction in terms. But when Marie asks whether he loves her, he talks only of his love for himself. She tries desperately to hold on to him, to keep him alive, but she becomes aware that he is forgetting her and soon, as he can no longer see her, she is made to disappear from our view, too.

Marguerite and the Doctor urge him to lighten the load and the style of this last sequence of the play is in some ways reminiscent of Choubert's psychological journey in *Victims of Duty*. There is a mirror in his entrails, he says, in which he can see more and more. He sees the world, he says, life slipping away. But beyond the reflection he sees only himself, beyond everything his own existence. Now Juliette suddenly vanishes, then the Doctor. He is alone with Marguerite, who helps him to lighten the load. His hearing is deteriorating, though he still hears her clearly as she tells him there are still some cords that bind him, some hands that cling to him, holding him back. Moving round him, she cuts the space as with an invisible pair of scissors.

Next she removes an invisible ball and chain from his feet and relieves him of an imaginary sack. She takes an invisible pack from his shoulders, repeating the same procedure for a spare pair of imaginary boots he has been carrying, a toolbox, a rusty sabre, thorns and splinters in his cloak, creepers and seaweed and slimy wet leaves all clinging to him. She helps him to straighten his hunched shoulders, to open the clenched fist in which he holds the whole Kingdom on microfilm, in tiny grains. Then she guides him across the stage before moving away from him, leaving him to walk by himself, to follow the flaming wheel in front of him without turning his head. Now he has nothing to fear.

He has lost all power of speech. He is hobbling towards the throne and she urges him on as he slowly climbs the steps. When she commands him to give her his legs, they stiffen, and one after another the parts of his body that she asks for become motionless until he is like a statue seated on the throne. Suddenly she too has vanished. The set indicating the throne room has also disappeared during this final sequence. There is nothing except Bérenger on his throne in the greying light. Then he too vanishes. The familiar process of proliferation has been reversed. Nothingness, which was also the subject of *The Chairs*, has been evoked in a totally different way. We have it now in front of us on the empty stage.

# Hunger and Thirst

The French text contains the description "play in three episodes" and though they are not entirely self-contained, they have very much less continuity than the three acts of an average three-act play. As Ionesco said in the interview, the second and third acts are concerned with different stages of questing. The first explores the marital and domestic situation which the man, Jean, leaves when he embarks on his quest. It could be seen as a development of a theme stated from the woman's point of view in A *Stroll in the Air,* when Josephine, in the nightmare sequence, shows her total devotion to Bérenger and her fear of the solitude she is left in without him. This theme has often appeared before: Amédée too flies away from his wife and, unlike Bérenger, does not return. The man in *Frenzy for Two* has already left his wife and during the action tries abortively to leave his mistress.

All this must obviously have its roots in Ionesco's childhood experience of seeing his mother abandoned by his father. Since then, he says in *Présent passé passé présent*[1], he has had pity, rightly or wrongly, for all women. He feels guilty towards them, having taken on his father's guilt. Fearing to make them suffer, he has let them make him suffer. And then he has made them suffer, and suffered himself from doing so. In *Hunger and Thirst* Jean's guilt at leaving Marie-Madeleine will accompany him through his quest.

Like *A Stroll in the Air* it is a play which both draws heavily on dreams and presents much of its action in a dreamlike form. Ionesco has told Claude Bonnefoy[2] how he made use of his dream about a woman in flames and his dream about a dead relation who visited him in very strange clothes. He talked about a dream he often has of a cellar in a house which may cave in. The cellar becomes identified with a tomb and his mother often appears in this dream. One version of this dream is also described in *Présent passé passé présent*.[3] He was living in ugly damp rooms similar to some that can be found in suburbs of Bucharest, and they moved into a dark basement where he felt very ill at ease, though he tried to console himself by saying that it didn't matter even if they lived in Bucharest—they could reach Paris in two minutes. But the darkness, damp, and ugliness of the two basement rooms were overwhelming. Then they had invited a crowd of people, including his father and his stepmother, who all stood there in the darkness, dressed in mackintoshes, cloaks, and overcoats. Waking up, he realized that the two basement rooms were graves and that the guests were mourners at a funeral. This also helps to explain the urge Jean feels in the first episode of the play to get away from the damp basement.

The atmosphere created at the beginning of the play is the opposite of that which opened *The Killer*, with its evocation of the radiant city. Exactly this kind of contrast to the present clammy ambiance is created by

Jean's opening speech. Why have they come back to live here again after the new house where they were before, with light coming in from all directions, and space stretching all around them? He talks about the dreams he has of a ghastly house, half sunk in the ground, half under water, oozing with mud, and he is convinced that this house too is sinking. His feeling of being starved of light and heat is elaborated at length, while Marie, the devoted wife, content with things as they are, points out that he always wants what he has not got. To her it seems beautiful. There is no central heating but she will warm the house with her heart; no electricity, but she will light it with her eyes. So long as she is with him and with their baby daughter she is not even afraid of dying. And she is convinced—rightly as it turns out—that he does not know how much he loves them. She even enjoys the beautiful shapes that the mildew makes on the walls, but he reads sinister meanings into them.

> To me they look like bleeding carcasses, heads bowed in sorrow, frightened people dying, mutilated bodies, with no head, no arms, fabulous monsters, prostrate, in pain, gasping for breath.

This is reminiscent of what Bérenger saw on his flight.

Before Aunt Adelaide comes in, she can be seen approaching in a mirror. She looks poverty-stricken and she is dressed in long veils, but she sits down naturally on the sofa and at first there is no clear indication that she is a ghost. Ionesco based her on his mother's sister, who, after a stroke, suffered from aphasia. She dressed like a pauper and begged in the streets. Finally she set fire to her own home and blamed it on the neighbor.[4] In the play she claims to have written the books on surgery and medicine that bear her husband's name.

She talks of the admirers that pursue her and believes that she still lives in her old home. She boasts that she writes the biographies of famous men, that she is the only one to know their secrets. She produces medals from her handbag to prove her importance. When Jean accuses her of setting fire to her house, she says it was the neighbor, who persecutes her, stealing into the house when she is out to pull the petals off flowers, one by one. Finally she exposes her breasts to prove that she is not a ghost and, taking out a knife, she makes a slit in her scalp to show that real blood is flowing.

This oppressive episode is followed almost immediately by the next oneiric reconstruction. When Marie speaks of lighting a fire, a chimney piece with a blazing fire appears either against the back wall or in the mirror. Jean sees a woman in the flames holding out her arms in agony, reproaching him. He imagines he could have saved her if he had dared to brave the flames. As soon as Marie addresses the phantom, exonerating her husband, the chimney piece and the flames vanish.

When he complains of hunger and thirst experienced simultaneously with a loss of appetite, no taste left for anything, she advises him to feed on desire and quench his thirst with hope. He must come to terms with his feelings of emptiness and feel fulfillment. With good enough eyesight you can see through the walls that block your view of the horizon.

The dialogue between them is followed by a series of alternating monologues during which she voices her preoccupations with him, the baby, the home, while he arrives at his decision to go away. He must harden his heart and be only himself. Reading his thoughts, she doubts whether he can pluck up his love for her by the roots, and this becomes the issue which is acted out in the remainder of this first episode. It starts playfully with a game of hide and seek. After several disappearances and reappearances, she sees him with his hat and gloves on, his overcoat over his arm. Her anxiety increases as the game cruelly continues. Desperately she tries to coax him to stop playing and stay. As they go on calling "cooeee" to each other, his voice becomes more and more distant. Again she says that he cannot tear this love from his heart, but now we see him tearing from his heart a branch of briar rose, wiping the blood on his shirt. When she finds the branch on the table and the trail of blood on the floor, she knows it is hopeless. But her self-pity is exceeded by her pity for the pain he must have felt.

Suddenly her remark about seeing through the walls is translated into visual terms. The back wall vanishes, revealing trees in blossom, luxuriant grass, a blue sky. Then a silver ladder is hanging in the air, its top invisible. If he had known all this was there, she says, he would not have abandoned them.

The second episode is set on a terrace that seems to be hanging in midair. The sky is dark, though it brightens the moment that Jean arrives. But it is an empty, shadowless brilliance, and there are arid mountains all round. Certainly this is the weakest of the three episodes. The two Keepers are the only characters for Jean to talk to and there is no valid dramatic reason for him to go on talking to them at such length. He becomes tiresome and garrulous in doing so. He chats on about his appreciation of the light, about his happiness at expecting her to arrive at any moment, about the museum he wants to show her. Everything he says is overstated and his eagerness becomes tedious. His certainty that she will come makes us quite certain that she won't, so that slender thread of suspense is soon very frayed.

When he asks the two Keepers to give her a message

from him, he finds he has forgotten her name and he cannot describe her. The Keepers are abnormally tolerant and interested in listening to his vague memories of the vague arrangements they have made for meeting. His confidence that he could not have torn the love from her heart echoes the image of Act One. He wanted to escape old age, he tells them, to keep out of the rut. He had to choose between peace and passion but now he regrets choosing passion.

> I was safe enough in my hideout, firmly locked in gloom and nostalgia, remorse and anguish, fears and responsibilities, like so many walls around me. The fear of death was my truest shield. Now the walls have collapsed. And here I am, defenseless, exposed to the blazing inferno of life, and in the freezing grip of despair. I wanted life and life has hurled itself at me. It's crippling me, killing me. Why didn't I have the sense to welcome resignation? All my old scars have opened, my wounds are bleeding again. Thousands of knives are driving into my flesh.

Basically, the whole act is a monologue like this, and the two Keepers are merely a stoogelike onstage audience. There is a slight variation when he thinks he sees a woman in the shadows and the Second Keeper disguises his voice to represent her. But it is not Marie. Now the light is fading and the museum is about to close. His references to the journey ahead suggest Ibsen and Strindberg at their most allegorical.

The final episode is set in the refectory of a monastery-cum-barracks-cum-prison. Through the bars in the gate at the back we see a dismal landscape but later when Marie and the fifteen-year-old Marthe enter, the bright garden that we saw at the end of Act One reappears. It is described by the stage directions as

Edenlike. So the subfusc walls of the refectory and the drab robes of the monks will help to suggest an image that was glimpsed in the dialogue of *The Chairs*—the image of being shut out from the Garden of Eden.

At first Jean, who seems older and exhausted, is made to feel very welcome. Brother Tarabas, the monks' spokesman, lets him think it is a resthouse for travelers. His feet are washed and he is given food and drink, though the appearance of the abnormally tall Brother Superior and of a monk with a carbine are vaguely disturbing.

When they ask what he has seen or heard on his travels, he seems unable to think of anything except the commonplace—people and meadows and houses and streams and railway lines and schoolchildren. They tell him he must have seen the ancient knight in armor, the palace, the crimson ocean, the chinks in the blue vault of heaven, the petrified hag, and the airy temples in space with pillars reaching down to earth. But he seems to remember nothing of all this. As his answers to their questions become more like individual words, they become more like schoolteachers, setting tests and awarding marks. The fog he complains of on the journey becomes one with the fog in his memory, but, under pressure from them, he recalls a ragged old woman leaning on a stick, standing still and staring at him. Without seeming to reach any conclusion, this sequence leads into an entertainment they offer him, a play about education and reeducation.

Two iron cages appear with two prisoners inside them, Tripp and Brechtoll. Two Brothers push carts loaded with food. More monks come on representing the audience. They are dressed in red on Brechtoll's side and in black on Tripp's. Both prisoners ask for their freedom but Tarabas inquires what do they want to be free from. Where they are, they are free from all attachment. Physical terror frees them from moral torment. They must free themselves from the idea of getting away and from their old habits of thought. He promises to disintoxicate them so that they will enjoy complete freedom. Their outlook will be different. They will be like the enlightened brothers, who have passed their apprenticeship in the art of unlearning. Aided by Tarabas, the Second and Third Brothers tempt the prisoners with food and when, eventually, they are both reduced to pleading for some, they are only teased, not given any. When Brechtoll asks them to have the goodness to give him some soup, he is told that he believes in goodness. When Tripp appeals to their charity he is told it would be humiliating for him if they fed him out of charity. Brechtoll claims to have demystified goodness—Ionesco often comes back ironically to this word "demystified"—Tripp is forced into saying that the Brothers have wronged him in imprisoning him but he holds back from saying they are wicked. He is very sure it was a mistake, he says, and their mistake is an error in their thinking.

In the same breath as pitying Brechtoll for not believing in God, Tarabas assures Tripp that they have no doctrines. Asked whether he wants to eat first or be released, Tripp chooses food first, only to be told that he has chosen to stay where he is, which proves that choice imprisons. Pleading for soup "for the love of God," it is only a step for Tripp to affirm his belief in God and to pray. But still he is not given any soup, and Brechtoll, who has stolidly refused to pray, is goaded first to the point where he exclaims "God, I'm hungry" and then into saying "Our Father, which art in heaven." He is now given soup but Tripp is told that because he believes in God he will not get any. Desperate now, he readily says that he does not believe in God.[5] The scene ends and Jean is told that in the next of the twenty-nine remaining episodes of the play, the two prisoners go off the idea of liberty. But Jean has no desire to see any more.

It is when he says he would like to be on his way that we are launched into the final sequence of the action. Waiting for the bill he has to settle, he tells them more about his journey. At one time everything was a source of wonder to him. The joy he took in what he saw relieved his hunger, slaked his thirst. But the luminous days came to an end and everything is hollow now. This is the familiar theme of the fall from the visionary paradise, familiar in Ionesco and a host of earlier writers, including the Wordsworth of *Intimations of Immortality*:

> —But there's a Tree, of many, one,
> A single Field which I have looked upon,
> Both of them speak of something that is gone:
> The Pansy at my feet
> Doth the same tale repeat:
> Whither is fled the visionary gleam?
> Where is it now, the glory and the dream?

Having no money to pay the monks what he owes them, Jean must discharge the debt morally. That he will have to stay on and work for them becomes clear at the same moment as Marie and Marthe appear outside the barred gate, waiting for him. The question of how long he will have to work and whether they will be able to wait is what gives suspense to the final sequence. The Tripp-Brechtoll episode has already eradicated the initial impression of benevolence the monks made. There have been hints of totalitarian methods in many of Tarabas's pronouncements: now he talks ominously of the way their surgeons have erased those germs of conflict which were ruining the monks' health. When he asks Jean whether he would like to work as a warder of the dungeon, it has the ring of an invitation to become a guard in a concentration camp. They settle that Jean's job will be waiting at table, but the Brother Accountant must work out how much time he owes them. We see him being dressed in a monk's habit and starting his work while the Brother Accountant calculates the number of hours of service which are due. As he mentions figures, the third Brother writes them on a blackboard, the other Brothers speak the numbers in chorus and they light up on screens all over the stage. Bowls and cutlery are being passed to Jean to the same rhythm, which increases as the numbers pile up, and this is still going on at an ever-increasing rate as the play ends.

Though the proliferation of the dishes takes us back to the style of earlier plays, the mood and the overall effect are very different. Ionesco has drawn on dreams ever since *Jacques*, in which the galloping stallion that caught fire was an oneiric image. What is different about the later plays is the way in which the dream material is developed. The stories tend to become more mythlike but at the same time the focus becomes less subjective. *The Bald Soprano* had very little to do with the external world and in *The Lesson* there was no attempt to integrate the reference to Nazism into the action. But from *The Killer* onwards Ionesco has been increasingly involved with public themes and the demonstration of brainwashing in *Hunger and Thirst* is equally relevant to religious and political conformism, which, as Ionesco suggests, are less different than they often appear.

The Tripp-Brechtoll episode stands out from the rest of the play, partly because it is so powerful, partly because it has so little to do with the central character. It is only relevant to Jean in that it demonstrates the methods of the people into whose hands he has fallen. Altogether the episodes into which Ionesco has divided the play tend to split up into smaller episodes. In the first act, the argument between Jean and Marie about the damp apartment is organically connected with the sequence about his decision to leave. Aunt Adelaide's episode has no organic connection with either, and the blazing woman episode has very little. This is one of the dangers of incorporating unedited oneiric material. The third act similarly has a central section, the Tripp-Brechtoll scene, which is not organically related either to what came before or to what comes after. Nor does the reappearance of Marie and Marthe link the end of the play very satisfactorily with the beginning. In any case, Jean is hardly the same person in Act Three as he was in Act One. If he is a character at all he has been characterized mainly by making him a direct mouthpiece for many of Ionesco's own preoccupations. Certainly this gives him a continuity of a sort but he does not develop at all meaningfully. If his journey is to have a cumulative dramatic significance, it must have the effect of changing him in some observable way. Although he does change, the changes do not seem to come as a result of the experience he undergoes and the pattern of changes never comes into focus. Ionesco frequently puts his feelings of the moment under the microscope, but seldom uses the telescope to see how far he has come.

# Killing Game

Killing Game, which received its first performance in January 1970,[1] was Ionesco's first play since Hunger and Thirst, which was performed in 1964. After the long silence it represents a brave new departure. It is the most ferocious of all Ionesco's plays and the one in which comedy is most closely intertwined with tragedy. I doubt whether any play has ever been written in which so many deaths occur, and partly because of their sheer quantity, they sometimes come close to comedy. The play has no central character, being made up of a series of nineteen short scenes, all involving different people and different stories within the general context of a plague. Like Camus's La Peste, it was inspired by Daniel Defoe's The Journal of the Plague Year. At first Ionesco had great difficulty in deciding how to end it. Finally he decided to kill off the survivors of the plague with a fire, because the Great Plague of 1665 was followed in 1666 by the Great Fire of London.

Defoe was only about five in 1665 and his book, published in 1722, was not altogether a factual reconstruction of what took place, though it affected the tone of objective reporting and incorporated a good deal of documentary material. The narrative is written from the viewpoint of a fictional resident in London who describes how the plague spread, causing growing panic. We learn about the measures taken by the civic authorities—what they did to isolate the victims, how they closed houses where the plague had struck and prohibited all meetings so as to reduce the scale of infection. There are graphic descriptions of the carts which went around London collecting the dead and of the burials in huge pits. The interruption of the city's commercial life is chronicled, together with other social and economic repercussions and statistics about the deaths.

All these ingredients are present in Ionesco's play, but unlike Defoe he has no interest in creating an impression of documentary verisimilitude. He is never concerned to attach a story to its historical or social context. Human life, for him, is a story which repeats itself endlessly, determined constantly by the all-important fact of mortality. And in *Killing Game* the references to both Paris and Berlin as ancient cities suggests that the action is intended to be taking place in the remote future, like that of *The Chairs*, though in neither play are there any indications of any development beyond that of today. And the stage directions in *Killing Game* suggest that the style should place it between 1880 and 1920.

But in many ways the mood is medieval. The proliferation of horrifying deaths suggests a canvas by Hieronymus Bosch, though neither the ubiquitous presence of the Black Monk nor the belief some of the characters have that their sins are the cause of their sufferings make it into a religious play. Ionesco may have had the image of Sodom and Gomorrah in his mind but the intention of his *danse macabre* is not to warn the audience about the perils of our disregarding God's will. It is rather to protest against the inevitability of death by firing a few more arrows at God's empty throne. "I wanted to go beyond the absurd, to underline the scandalous aspect of death—an elementary truth that people know but dismiss too readily."[2] So for the first time in Ionesco's work, the two themes of death and proliferation are united; now it is death that proliferates. But despite the copresence of these two hallmarks, for someone who arrived at a performance without knowing who the author was, it would not be easy to guess.

It is written for a huge cast but the stage directions suggest that some of the citizens could be represented by large marionettes, or dolls, or painted figures. The city is intended to be a large one: we know from the dialogue that it has at least twenty-seven arrondissements and a population of over 800,000. If some of the citizens sound provincial, that has nothing to do with living in the provinces any more than bourgeois attitudes have to do with belonging to the middle class.

The set will be adapted for various interior scenes but basically it represents a main square in the city where there is a marketplace. The conversation of the housewives about disease and the dangers of different foods quickly moves beyond naturalism. Unwashed carrots can cause leprosy, we hear, and mussels can be the cause of the plague. So the word is introduced, comically, within the first two minutes.

After a series of fragments of female conversation, we get a series of fragments of male conversation, still without any of the characters becoming more important than the others. Some of these scraps of dialogue restate familiar Ionesco themes, while others create comedy almost in the style of a revue sketch, as in the very brief conversation when the Third Man, who is pushing twins in a baby carriage, says that he always does this on Sunday while his wife knits. The Fourth Man says that for him it is the other way around. One man suggests to another that he could solve his problems by hanging himself. He rejects this idea as too dangerous but he is soon saying that perhaps it would be better to be dead.

Sometimes the women start talking rhythmically in chorus, almost like the Uncles and Aunts in T. S. Eliot's *The Family Reunion*. But the presence of the Black Monk, tall and cowled, who moves in and out unseen among the market shoppers, is more ominous than any formalization of speech. It is the sudden realization that the twins have gone blue which starts the main action. Asked to look after them while the two men go for a quick drink, two of the women soon realize they are dead. Accusing his mother-in-law of having killed them, the father rushes at her and she falls dead, though he has not even touched her. Another man draws a knife on him and he too falls dead, though not from the knife. Another woman collapses while calling for the police and another who is about to call the fire brigade. As the corpses go on piling up on the stage, the survivors first quarrel, then try to run away. By the end of this short scene we have seen sixteen deaths.

The next scene consists of a long speech by a local government official who uses the phrase "geometrical progression" of death—the same phrase that was used about the growing corpse in *Amédée*. He announces that the city is now surrounded by soldiers; no one can enter or leave. He asks for volunteers to bury the dead and announces measures very similar to those Defoe described for segregating victims so as to minimize the dangers of infection. Citizens should denounce their fellow citizens whenever there is reason to suspect the infection, and red crosses are to be painted on the doors of houses that are sealed off, together with the inscription "God have pity on us."

The first indoor scene is prefaced by the spectacle of two men with masks on their faces and knives in their gloved hands pursuing a half-naked man who is crying for mercy. We also see a woman in rags who says she has killed her child and we see police sealing off an infected house. In this play Ionesco never narrows his focus for long. Individual characters are not developed so as to interest us in their own right. He is concerned only with their behavior and with that only as part of a panorama.

Inside the house a master is ordering his servants to spray everything with disinfectant. But his reference to "the oil that prevents the scourge" suggests a primitive rather than technological society, though he also refers to "insecticides." As in *Exit the King*, the anachronisms are deliberate, though they are arguably less justified here because it is patently untrue that all societies would cope with the plague in the same way. One of the merits of Camus's *La Peste* was that it exploited the twentieth-century background.

By his fussiness and the pettiness which shows through his anxiety, the master of the house becomes more of a character than anyone else has so far, though this is mainly because he simply has more to say. In any case the characterization, like the curious ritual he makes his servants go through of declaring that they are "impenetrable," is only an elaboration of the build-up to the predictable climax—the revelation that he is himself infected. The police prevent the servants from leaving the house.

The scene in the clinic is the first in which the characters are given names. Alexander, an elderly man in his sixties, is in bed. With him are his much younger wife, Katya, and two slightly younger visitors, Jacques and Emile, who has not seen him for twenty years because of a quarrel. As Emile says, the hardest thing to forgive in other people is their having different ideas from your own. For two men to stay friends their ideas should change at the same rate, and Emile implies it might not have been coincidence that they quarreled the day after he received a literary prize that Alexander deserved more than he did. Just as the doctor is expressing doubt of whether the plague can be termed a "disease," Alexander dies, and not from the illness for which he was being treated.

Back in the street we see a meeting between two citizens, one of whom comes from a district which has been very badly hit, though the other, a resident of the most fashionable district, has persuaded the city council to rule that people should not have access to less affected districts. Snobbishly confident that the high level of sanitation on the social level where he lives must make him quite safe from infection, he thinks that all he needs to do is keep his distance from his less fortunate fellow citizen and buy his food in the best shops. His complacency is soon upset when he is told that the man he had dinner with last night has since died. Now it is the other citizen who is asking him to keep his distance. By the end of the scene we know that neither of them, nor the nurse who is called to examine them, will survive.

In the prison scene we see a warden telling two convicts that they are free. Thanks to the thickness of the prison walls, they are safer inside than outside, but so many of the wardens are dead that they can make their own choice about whether to stay. One of them has had a dream about piles of corpses higher than a six-story building so he decides to stay. Suddenly introducing the theme of politics, the other prisoner says that his party needs him, so he decides to go, only to be killed immediately, as the rats get him. The dream seems to have prompted the right decision but with an abrupt burst of gratuitous violence, the warden who had seemed so benevolent shoots the survivor and hangs himself. As in the opening scene, we see a murderous violence coming in the wake of other people's deaths, but here, as there, there is something slightly hard to take about this moment. Ionesco may be right or partly right to believe that fear of death is a motive for killing others but just as he tends to simplify the connection when he is arguing in general terms, he seems slightly to force the connection in his drama. It looks as though incidents are being coerced into a pattern of development in order to illustrate a theory.

So far no character has appeared in more than a single scene but now Emile and Jacques reappear in a street, meeting Pierre. Like the superior bourgeois, they all talk disparagingly of the poor districts as if it were only there that the plague was rampant. They try to convince themselves that Alexander's death was not a result of the epidemic, but the conversation founders when Pierre falls down dead.

This is followed by a very brief street scene in which one passer-by describes a case of multiplication among the dead: after leaving a room in which there were two bodies he returned a few minutes later to find eleven.

For the next scene the stage is divided into two halves, both representing interiors. On one side a woman, Jeanne, is receiving a man, Jean: on the other Lucienne is receiving Pierre (not the same Pierre). For the first part of the sequence the dialogue on both sides is identical, though not simultaneous. Jeanne puts a question to Jean and before he answers Lucienne has put the same question to Pierre. Then Jean's answer is echoed by Pierre's. Both men have been outside the city but have slipped past the guards to come back to their wives. Both couples talk about the present situation and about the past, when they were happy but did not know it. Then on one side Jeanne is taken ill, while on the other Pierre is. The dialogue is still very nearly parallel, but now Pierre repeats what Jeanne has just said while Lucienne echoes Jean. As usual, the condition of the victims deteriorates rapidly, but Jeanne dies in Jean's arms while Lucienne runs away from Pierre, ignoring his appeals that she should stay.

The following scene is also played on a divided set, this time without any echoing of dialogue. The action is very simply contrived so that there is silence on one side while dialogue is in progress on the other. A socialite mother is helping her daughter to get ready for a secret ball where she will meet her fiancé, while a traveler arrives at an inn. On one side the daughter dies and on the other the traveler. The two deaths are discovered simultaneously.

In the night scene which follows this one, we see a house with five windows. Scenes are going on in each of them which partly overlap. After the first one lights up we hear a cry for help. In the second room there is a father who has hanged himself. The son tries to revive him with oxygen. The old man in the third has taken out a revolver and holds it to his temple. In the fourth an old woman is calling out for help as a nurse advances menacingly on her, wanting to strangle her to get her money. In the fifth a man in pajamas is telling them to be quiet as he has to go to work in the morning. By the end of the scene the police have tried to seal off the house but the woman has jumped out of the first window into the street, the old man has shot himself and fallen out, and the police are deciding to finish them all off with a machine gun.

The next scene is a continuation of this one. Two of the policemen have been inside the house to shoot everyone. Outside they are both examined for symptoms and the one who is found to be infected is shot by the others.

Most of the following scene, the thirteenth, is given to a political speech by an orator who, like Botard in *Rhinoceros*, politicizes everything, seeing a plot in the plague. It is a means of keeping the people down. It is a mystery which must be demystified—Ionesco still has not tired of this phrase. He takes the opportunity to introduce some statistics: up to two days ago there had been 190,000 deaths, nearly a quarter of the population, but of the twenty-one members of the city council four are outside the city's boundaries while only three have died, and all three were opponents of the dominant party. The Orator inflames the crowd to enthusiasm for the absurd program of action he puts forward— killing the lackeys of the regime who are going around collecting the dead. But when the Orator falls down dead himself, the gullible crowd considers him to be a martyr of the cause.

The political orator in the next scene is more moderate but he blames the council for setting such a bad example in letting three of its members die. He promises a healthier government.

The next scene shows us a meeting of some male and female doctors, who speak in general terms about death. The majority of them, like Ionesco, seems to think that death is unnatural and should be resisted. Most of them implicitly deny all evidence of the reality of the plague and at one point, to stress the nonsensicality of their dialogue, Ionesco makes them break into song like the characters in *A Stroll in the Air*. People who die are bad citizens, they sing, insufficiently politicized. At the end they all fall down dead.

The most sympathetic characters in the whole play are the old couple who appear next: like Marie in *Hunger and Thirst*, the old woman is capable of enjoying everything she sees. Unlike her and like Jean, the old man has been unable to keep his sense of wonder intact. All his life he has been waiting to live but there is nothing to wait for now except nothingness. But for her, the love she feels towards him is a constant means of self-renewal. He says he can love no one, then contradicts himself by saying he still loves her, because he needs her. The first part of the scene is written too much in terms of statement. Both of them are just saying what they feel, though it is interesting when he says that he cannot bear being shut up in this city or in their house. He has come to hate the hearth. This speech links the claustrophobia of this play, set in a city virtually under siege, with the claustrophobia of Act One of *Hunger and Thirst*. In both plays Ionesco seems to be identifying with characters who feel imprisoned in an ambiance where death will come to them if they cannot get away. But this scene, like so many scenes in *Killing Game*, does not really get going until illness supervenes. It is the old woman who is dying and now their attempts to reassure each other are very touching. By the end of the scene they are both dead.

The next scene, an insert which does not appear in the Gallimard edition but which was included in the Paris production, is the most horrifying of all. It starts with a confrontation between an unsympathetic local government official and a group of women complaining of starvation and protesting about the rule that supplies are not to be shared between one district and another. Then one of the women tries to steal another's baby in order to eat it. A man knifes her to steal it from her while the other women steal her corpse to eat that. Developing this new-found theme of famine and cannibalism, Ionesco brings on a woman selling patés of human meat in the street and a man who lures another to his house by offering to sell him a pair of boots for two pieces of bread. On arriving the victim is knifed. The scene ends with people trying to steal bodies off the funeral cart and with a policeman chasing a man who is carrying two human heads. This is followed by a scene in which women are seen plundering an abandoned shop, and then by the final scene, in which the announcement that the plague is over is followed by a wild outburst of joy from the survivors. But it only lasts until they see that they are already surrounded by a fire which is obviously going to annihilate them.

*Killing Game* is not an appealing play. Deliberately Ionesco keeps us at a distance from all the characters except for our brief moment of involvement at the end of the scene with the old couple. But it is an important play, not only because he is breaking so courageously away from his normal dramatic vocabulary but because he succeeds in incarnating his vision three-dimensionally and dynamically. In plays like *A Stroll in the Air* and *Hunger and Thirst*—with the exception of isolated episodes like Josephine's nightmare and the brainwashing sequence—too much of what he has to say is said simply by putting it into the mouth of the main character, while making only secondary use of the medium's visual potentialities. Here, although the themes and preoccupations are the same, he has started formally almost from scratch. The division of the play into very short scenes offers a new solution to the problem of intermissions. Ionesco shows very considerable skill in contriving so much variation and comedy in scenes that nearly all have the same ending as the characters fall down dead. The play also provides an effectively panoramic view of a stricken society which he sees as differing from our own only in the speed of the incidence of death.

The most serious flaws in the play have, I think, three main roots: the denial of the relevance of historical factors, the attempt to dispense with a central story and with a central character, and the stubborn immaturity of the attitude toward death. The basic assumption, as usual, is that death is the root of all evil, and that everything in the world would improve if only God could be persuaded to change his mind about mortality.

# Macbett

Alfred Jarry's 1896 play *Ubu Roi* was to be seminal over half a century later in the vogue for grotesquely tragic farces that started in the nineteen-fifties. Inspired partly by the memory of a tyrannous schoolmaster and partly by *Macbeth*, Jarry's play inflated Shakespeare's tragic hero into a comic monster, a foul-mouthed clown who is egged on by his harridan wife into murdering the King of Poland and goes on to massacre all the noblemen in the country for the sake of money and food to stuff into his ever-expanding gut. Jarry was 23 when he wrote his play, which is less polemical than iconoclastic, a play that could only have been written by a very young man. *Macbett*, published in 1973, also makes *Macbeth* into a clown show, but it is written as if Ionesco's memories of *Ubu* had sunk into his unconscious mind. "Never have I written about such sinister themes with such pleasure," he reports in a program note. "It was as if I was dancing on tens of thousands of corpses and on whole countries that were ravaged by flood and fire as they are all around us." Jarry was conscious of the outrageousness of his youthful dance; at sixty Ionesco was dancing less exuberantly, more conscious of being outraged at the realities of *realpolitik* and the impossibility of exaggerating the monstrosity of political action.

*Macbeth* also had an appeal for Ionesco which had nothing to do with the machinery of the state or with Jarry. "*Macbeth*, or Death-Infected" is Jan Kott's title for his chapter on the play in *Shakespeare Our Contemporary*,[1] and of all Shakespeare's plays this yields the clearest patterns of proliferation. After killing Duncan, Macbeth goes on to kill the groom outside his room. Banquo is next to be murdered, then Lady Macduff and her son. As Kott points out, "There is more and more blood, everyone walks in it; it floods the stage." One killing leads to the next until Macbeth is ready to kill everybody not prepared to fight against his enemies: "Hang those that talk of fear."

Reviewing Ionesco's *Macbett* in *Le Monde*[2], Bertrand Poirot-Delpech saw in it a departure from some thirty plays "patently inspired by his private fantasies. It is the first time that Ionesco has projected onto external phenomena in a play a belief in systematic pattern . . . *Macbett* expresses an argument, reflects a considerable scheme, supports a thesis." But while it may seem to be putting forward a view of history, it is nonsocial and nonpolitical. The ideas and the imagery are in line with those of *Killing Game*. This time the wholesale slaughter is kept offstage, but again Ionesco is looking quizzically through the wrong end of the telescope at events that could seem tragic in close-up. He makes Macbett say:

> Tens of thousands of men, women, and children are dead, suffocated in cellars beneath the wreckage of their homes, blown up on orders from me.

Hundreds of thousands died as they tried in panic to cross the Channel and drowned. Millions died of terror or committed suicide. Tens of millions of others died of anger, apoplexy or grief. Not enough land left to bury them all. The bloated bodies of the drowned have soaked up all the water of the lakes in which they threw themselves. No more water. Not enough vultures to rid us of all this carrion flesh. And to think there are still some left who go on fighting! There must be an end to it. If their heads are sliced off, fountains of blood spring from their throats to drown my own soldiers too.

The multiplication is mechanical, and whereas Shakespearean battles are always fought with right on one side and wrong on the other, Ionesco postulates a Duncan, a Macbett, a Banco and a Macol (Malcolm) who are equally reprehensible. In all Shakespeare's histories, in *As You Like It* and in *The Tempest*, as in *Macbett*, the polarity is between the good ruler and the bad ruler. The bad ruler is always a usurper, and the rightful heir to the throne returns triumphantly in the final scene, restoring peace and justice to a ravaged state. In *Macbett* the Scottish people are no worse off under Macbett than they were under Duncan, and they will be no better off under Macol. Ionesco's final *coup de théâtre* is to have Macol repeat Malcolm's speech from Act IV, Scene 3.

Better Macbett than such a one to reign. With this, there grows in my most ill-composed affection, such a staunchless avarice, that, were I king, I should cut off the nobles for their lands; desire his jewels, and this other's house: and my more-having would be as a sauce to make me hunger

more; that I should forge quarrels unjust against
the good and loyal, destroying them for wealth.
The king-becoming graces, as justice, verity, tem-
perance, stableness, bounty, perseverance, mercy,
lowliness, devotion, patience, courage, fortitude,
I have no relish of them; but abound in the
division of each several crime, acting it many ways.

But whereas Malcolm was testing Macduff's loyalty
to Scotland by painting a false picture of himself,
Macol is telling the undisguised truth, and the play
ends after the frightened courtiers have slunk away to
leave him alone on stage. History repeats itself endlessly
as one unjust, untruthful, intemperate, unstable tyrant
exploits the power he has wrested from his unjust, untruthful, intemperate, unstable predecessor. Starting the
story much earlier than Shakespeare, Ionesco shows
that the reasons Glamiss and Candor have for rebelling
against the Archduke Duncan are no less valid than
the grievances that will later accrue against Macbett.

If Shakespeare's love of stability and fear of civil
disorder are conservative, Ionesco's views are dia-
metrically opposed, without being radical. The revolutionary's premise is that social justice is attainable. For
Ionesco, there is no value in overturning the established
order, not because it is good, but because any alternative is equally undesirable. "All dictators become
paranoiacs," Ionesco wrote in the program note. "The
world will be peaceful only when we are no longer
ruled by the state."

He points up the moral sameness of his characters by
pairing them and letting them echo each other. Banco
is like Macbett's twin brother—Lady Duncan mistakes
one for the other—while Glamiss is like Candor's twin.
Their denunciation of Duncan is not so much a dialogue
as a monologue split between two voices.

> GLAMISS: I have my own people. My own army.
> They are my own men that he could turn
> against me.
> CANDOR: Against me too.
> GLAMISS: Never seen the like.
> CANDOR: Never, never since my forebears . . .
> GLAMISS: And my forebears too.
> CANDOR: And all his followers, rummaging and
> foraging about.
> GLAMISS: Getting fat on the sweat of *our* brows.
> CANDOR: On the fat of *our* fowls.
> GLAMISS: *Our* sheep.
> CANDOR: And *our* swine.

Sometimes Ionesco uses repetition and verbal patterning to emphasize the pairing between characters.
After Macbett finishes the long speech from which I
quoted, Banco appears and makes the same speech.
There is a pair of witches, instead of a trio, and the
grievances against Duncan that are first voiced by the
rebels are repeated verbatim by the two Witches when
they are tempting Macbett and Banco to kill the Archduke, and then, again verbatim, by Macbett and Banco
themselves. Far from being more loyal than Macbett,
Banco strikes the first blow. Needing no exemplars of
moral uprightness, Ionesco dispenses with Macduff
altogether.

The basic idea for the play is an interesting one but
Ionesco is again trying to hold a precarious balance between tragedy and farce, without succeeding to the
extent that he did in *Exit the King.* The main difficulties derive partly from having to reshape another
playwright's material, partly from having to crowd in
so much physical action. He does achieve a series of
remarkable theatrical impacts, often by inverting Shakespearean points, and sometimes by introducing new

material. The script is rich in the comic opportunities it offers the actors, but it is almost impossible for the director to integrate the parodistic and the serious elements. While the cosmic imagery in *Exit the King* was suggestive of Shakespearean tragedy in general and *Macbeth* in particular, it focused attention on a real physical universe outside the theatrical hero; the universe of *Macbett* is entirely artificial and the characters never become real enough to move or involve us. When they talk about the enormous toll of human suffering taken by warfare and tyranny, they sound like catalogs, and when they echo each other they sound like comedians. Yet the play cannot work unless we take their actions seriously. Ionesco has also stripped away all Shakespeare's poetry, providing nothing to replace it except stage directions asking for spectacular visual effects reminiscent of *A Stroll in the Air* and *Hunger and Thirst*.

A lot of the comedy is schoolboyish. Candor tiptoes up behind Banco with his sword unsheathed, preparing to kill him, and changes his mind at the last minute. There are puns like the one about pancakes from China (*crêpes de Chine*), tired anachronistic jokes like the references to television, and the Archduke's younger son, Donalban, is taking a diploma at Ragusa in Economics and the Art of Navigation. On the other hand there is some very shrewd theatrical exploitation of the basic idea. While Shakespeare's Macbeth is almost unsoldierly in his qualms about killing, the two Witches are aptly able to tempt Macbett to murder Duncan by arguing that he has never previously had any compunction about killing when given the order. Unlike Shakespeare's Duncan, Ionesco's is a flagrantly unjust ruler. He breaks his promises and has a messenger beheaded for bringing bad news. Killing him, therefore, is no worse than killing the innocent on his behalf. And as the first Witch tells Macbett, if he weren't so useful to Duncan, his own neck would have been in danger.

The scene with the Wounded Soldier closely parallels Shakespeare's scene with the bleeding sergeant, but Ionesco amusingly makes his soldier uncertain of which side he's been fighting on. He was enlisted by a sergeant on horseback who lassooed him. When Duncan finds out that he was fighting for the rebels, Lady Duncan almost executes him on the spot, but bathetically relents because he's so polite. The closest approximation to the wholesale death of *Killing Game* occurs when a whole series of guillotines appear and tea is served with cakes while Banco presses the button to release the blades. In rapid succession the heads of the rebels drop into a basket, while Lady Duncan keeps count, arriving at the figure 9,300 in the same breath as 300, and at 20,000 only a couple of seconds later.

There is no Lady Macbett but the two Witches do all the necessary tempting, transforming themselves from old hags into the doubles of Lady Duncan and the attractive young Gentlewoman who acts as her Lady-in-Waiting. In the form of Lady Duncan the first Witch offers to become Macbett's mistress as soon as he has killed the Archduke, also making him the Shakespearean promise that none born of woman shall vanquish him and that his army will not be defeated until Birnam Wood marches against him. The murder of Duncan comes at the climax of the one sequence in which we see him doing good, looking "truly majestic" in the presence of a Monk as he successfully uses his "gift of divine grace" to cure "the scrofulous, the phlegmonic, the consumptive and the hysterical." In an accelerating procession, eleven patients recover immediately after receiving the royal treatment, but then the Monk turns out to be Banco wearing a hood or mask and hiding a long dagger under his cowl, while the twelfth and thirteenth patients reveal themselves as Macbett and Lady Duncan.

In Shakespeare's play the murder is committed in the second of the five acts; in Ionesco's it comes when four-fifths of the play is over, and in the fifth that remains, his control over his material grows increasingly slack. The equivalent to Shakespeare's banquet scene is very weak. Ionesco is undecided whether Duncan's first appearance should be represented by a portrait or an empty frame. Before Banco's ghost appears, Macbett embarrasses his sycophantic guests by asking them, rather overexplicitly, whether they ever told Duncan that in their opinion he was less suited to the throne than his General, and when Duncan's ghost proceeds to install himself on the throne in the banqueting room, he is rather too explicit in admitting how much damage he has done to the country. As in *A Stroll in the Air*, Ionesco arbitrarily asks for certain passages of dialogue to be sung operatically, and, after exchanging insults with Macbett, Macol has a passage, which may either be spoken or sung in a Wagnerian style, revealing that Duncan was only his adoptive father. His real father was Banco; his mother was a gazelle, temporarily transformed by witchcraft into a woman. He will take the name of Banco II and his dynasty will reign for centuries. In an apparition we see the heads of Banco III, Banco IV and Banco V, who look like characters from a French cartoon strip, and Banco VI, who looks like Ionesco. For the Birnam Wood episode Ionesco wants to give the impression that the whole of the decor is advancing threateningly on Macbett, but it is left to the director to find the best technical effect he can. Ionesco's suggestion is that men and women should converge on Macbett carrying placards with trees or branches drawn on them. Macol's final speech could be very effective theatrically, but the play ends with a Butterfly Collector crossing the stage, net in hand. He wears a boater and pince-nez. He has been seen once before when the stage was empty between two episodes involving the Witches. The irrelevance is deliberate, but unhelpful.

# The Mire, The Hermit,
and *What a Hell of a Mess!*

Solitude is the subject both of Ionesco's film
*La vase* (1970–71), derived from his 1956 story entitled *The Mire,* and of his play *What a Hell of a Mess!*
(1973), derived from his novel *The Hermit,* which
appeared earlier the same year. Both narratives are
written in the first person; in both adaptations the
central figure is nameless, described as "The Character." In both narratives the bulk of the action is
internal; so in both adaptations the main problem is
exteriorizing it. And with the film—perhaps Ionesco
was unfamiliar with the medium—remarkably few new
elements are introduced.

The plot of the film *La vase* follows the short story
very closely, even retaining the same supporting characters, all of very minor importance. The same contrast
is drawn between vernal and wintry landscape, though
the effect is, of course, very different when the medium
is visual. The appearance of fog on the screen makes
an impact quite unlike that of the phrase "a sort of
mental fog." Ionesco kept a stubborn grip on the

images of his fourteen-year-old story: a headless frog jumps into the picture because the narrator of the story has compared the functioning of his reflexes with those of a decapitated frog. The film sequence showing the Character's narrow escape from being knocked down by a truck originates in the much less dramatic observation "Several times I narrowly escaped being knocked down on the road by trucks whose noise sounded to me like a light breeze caressing my ears."

There are relatively few words in the film and naturally they are less important in relation to the visual elements than in any of Ionesco's plays. The key phrases all come straight out of the story:

> I intend to make my contribution to the betterment of the human race. Man's fate is far from perfect, besides I notice I have a liver.

> I've made up my mind to make up my mind.

> My overcoat's not waterproof. Nor is my hat.

> Ah! If the dampness was warmer . . . it would be perfect.

In Ionesco's work there is a sharp contrast between the plays (like the Bérenger sequence and *Hunger and Thirst*) in which he identifies strongly with the central character, using him partly as a mouthpiece, and those (like *The Bald Soprano* and *The Lesson*) in which all the characters are viewed with comic detachment. In this respect both *Killing Game* and *Macbett* revert to the manner of his early work—there is no more identification with Macbett than with Banco or Duncan. But in many obvious ways the Character in *La vase* and *What a Hell of a Mess!* is Ionesco. In the film he played the part himself, and after it was shown in England at Oxford he told interviewer Melinda Camber[1] "The character was a part of myself that I'd freed myself from."

The disembodied eye that ends the film he explained as a symbol of awareness "and I hope that is what I bring to my readers." As he said, he depends on the response he receives from the readers for reassurance that he is not alone. He continues:

> Of course, there is the problem of solitude. It is a death within life. But isolation is different from solitude. In my solitude, when I am writing I meditate and regain equilibrium. I leave behind the social being, the inessential, to find the universal being. Real conversation does not take place in social gatherings or even between two people. It exists via the medium of work. It is difficult to communicate, but it is not impossible. I believe that the language of a writer can break through the incommunicability implicit in language.[2]

The pattern in *La vase* is a fairly simple one. The first words of the story are "I was in the prime of life"; the first words in the film are "Once upon a time my waking up used to be a moment of triumph." We see Ionesco dashing downstairs, striding rapidly along a road, busily writing letters and tucking them into envelopes that pile up at great speed. (The character in the story writes forty-four letters a day.) But very soon the bodily mechanism appears to run down as the spring landscape abruptly turns wintry. His face ages visibly and he goes unshaven, his hair grows white, his room becomes untidy. The plate of soup on the table in front of him is transformed into a murky pool, the salad turns into thorns. We are given surreal views of his anatomy—a furry tongue, a liver imperialistically push-

ing stomach and intestines out of its way. The sound
effects blur as if he is going deaf, and we hear a broken
down version of the song he used to sing cheerfully.
He sinks apathetically into lethargy, sleeps in his
clothes, stops answering the door. Letters that are
pushed under it accumulate on the floor. Weeks go by.
The passage of time is registered by alternate shots of
what he sees with his eyes open and closed: his worn
armchair with a newspaper and a dirty plate on the
floor beside it; a dark wheel rotating around a glowing
hub that diminishes in size.

The turning point comes when he wakes up panic-
stricken in the middle of the night and decides to pull
himself together "I've made up my mind to make up
my mind." He pictures himself functioning actively
again and when the dawn comes, tries to resume his old
routine. Recognizing a division in himself between the
impulse to go on and the inclination to let it all slide,
he pushes himself wearily forward. In both the story and
the film we are reminded of Beckett by the sequence
in which he struggles into his clothes and totters weakly
into a muddy landscape, but the comedy lacks Beckett's
sureness of touch. As the Character walks along he tries
to cheer himself up by thinking about the people he
will soon see, the sub-prefect he knew at school, and his
cheerful friends in the grocery shop. The puddles and
the mud become symbolic of what we sink into unless
other people drag us out, and after a man passes in his
cart without offering help, the Character falls into the
mud and makes himself comfortable in it. "Ah! If the
dampness was warmer . . . it would be perfect." He tries
to think about nothing, to empty his mind, and soon he
is unconscious. Coming to, he struggles to his feet and
with great difficulty makes his way forward, searching
for the road he used to know. He squelches depressively

through the mud until his legs give way beneath him, and, settling back into it, remarks that he's no worse off. He talks deprecatingly of "this nostalgia for everything, for life." Fleeting memories of his past are represented by a succession of images, and the sound of leaves "moaning" under the pattering rain is counterpointed against shots of brightly lit shops and laughing children playing games. Stretched out in the mud, the Character is uncertain whether his past experience was anything more than a dream. Or perhaps he was living through memories that belonged to someone else. Suddenly he is climbing up an arid mountainside with bleeding hands, but he tumbles into a well-watered country to find himself on his back again. He remembers his childhood, uncertain of where he came from or whether he has always been where he is.

His body starts to disintegrate. The right arm sinks into the mud. His liver presses against his lung. Skin splits, bones crack. A fleeting image of a woman in a shoe shop confuses him. His mother or his wife? The other arm, the hips, the abdomen drop off. The heartbeat grows infrequent. "I am more than pure lucidity, a conscious mind that registers . . ." he tells himself. Nothing remains except his head, and then nothing except his eye. His words remain optimistic, promising to start all over again, and as the eye vanishes the sky is blue.

As Ionesco told Melinda Camber,

> Death is our main problem. But the ignorance of ourselves and of others to which we are condemned is just as worrying. In the final analysis we don't know what we're doing. . . . Love was absent from the film, not because I believe that it is irrelevant but rather because that was the core of

the character's problem. He had no one to help
him live. Without love the world is unbearable.
. . . That's another reason why I don't believe in
revolution. It is a venting of hatred, rather than
love.[3]

It is out of the same preoccupations that *The Hermit*
and *What a Hell of a Mess!* emerge. Both love and
revolution are represented in the plot, but the Character enters into no satisfying contacts with other people,
who remain (as Ionesco put it in the program note for
the Paris production) "living enigmas." Besides, the
whole universe is an enigma for him, and he despairs
at not having the key to it. He does not achieve *com-
prehension*. Most people settle for a partial understanding which doesn't clear up our fundamental ignorance.
Unable to make do with that, the Character is constantly aware that the world has been made badly, that
it is ravaged by unhappiness and evil, that the different political and historical aspects of this evil are no
more than scarcely differentiated repetitions of a basic
tragedy. So he lives without being able to live in this
existential malaise, tortured every minute, astonished,
stupefied at what happens.

"Alcohol isn't enough to brutalize him and his
astonishment remains intact. But this astonishment,
which makes him suffer, is at the same time his salva-
tion. He observes the world with an innocent eye, on
the far side of all questions of 'why' and 'how.' "

*The Hermit* is nearly six times as long as the short
story *The Mire* and the action is less physical, more
mental. The novel retails the narrator's ideas and attitudes in great detail and they correspond very closely
with those of Ionesco, who this time would not be able
to say that the character was a part of himself that he'd
freed himself from. The Character, though, is not a

writer but a clerk who retires when he inherits a fortune, and the first-person narrative blurs the frontier Ionesco has tried to define between isolation and solitude. Unable to regain equilibrium in the meditational solitude of writing, the Character cannot escape the social being and the inessential. But neither can he accept them.

Beckett has sometimes had the same problem of explaining why his central characters could not derive the same satisfaction as other people do from the normal social and sexual activities. In the 1938 novel *Murphy* the hero hates the part of himself that craves for the prostitute who loves him and he loves the part that shrivels at the thought of her. In *Krapp's Last Tape* the old man looks ironically back at his "flagging pursuit of happiness" on licensed premises. "Unattainable laxation" he calls it. Even his childhood memories are unhappy ones, like Malone's in *Malone Dies*: "I was already in the toils of earnestness. That has been my disease. I was born grave as others syphilitic."[4] Ionesco's rhythms and images are more pedestrian than Beckett's, and the depressions and withdrawals of his narrator in *The Hermit* are more prosaic than Murphy's, Krapp's or Malone's, but both the rhythms and the sentiments are reminiscent of Beckett, as when the narrator compares himself with the people who do not experience their own desires strongly enough to entertain a real wish for them to detonate into fulfilment. "Good, the desire for women is dead. For ever, I hope. Besides I never wanted them much. That's what saved me from women but I still want to drink wine."[5] He feels morose most of the time, he says, perhaps because he has spent too long on reading newspapers. He feels ill at ease inside his own skin and he is troubled by the idea of infinity. He feels that his body is a heavy, disagreeable organism which at once is and is not his self.

In the gray interior spaces there is nothing but rubble underneath more rubble.

Does Ionesco want us to regard his Character as typical or exceptional? Or does his main impetus come from the compulsion to create self-portraits in the hope of receiving expressions of solidarity? At the beginning of the novel he makes his first-person narrator say he is sceptical, disillusioned, tired, living without an objective, and doing a minimum of work, "like everybody else today." But he is exceptional in withdrawing so fully from human contacts—partly voluntarily, partly involuntarily.

The starting point for the action in both the novel and the play is a legacy from an uncle in America. Suddenly rich, he has no reason to go on working in an office, and there is little else to distract him from the vacuum. He is not yet forty but he has gone for five years without making love. The sight of pregnant mothers pushing baby carriages and young fathers holding children by the hand makes him feel either homicidal or suicidal, and we are told in deliberately tedious detail how he passes the time, watching murder films, window shopping and, without even liking coffee, drinking cup after cup in cafés. He resents the aggressive noise of motorbikes and he feels occasional surges of happiness, which aren't strong enough. Reading the novel, we feel alternate surges of sympathy and irritation. He often slips into philosophizing, apologetically expressing the wish that he had more talent for it. Not being able to conceive the inconceivable is itself inconceivable, he maintains, speculating about the creation and pondering the necessity for resignation.

Halfway through the book he laconically announces (inside a parenthesis) that he intends to make or resume contact with other people. Structurally this is a pivot equivalent to the decision halfway through *The*

*Mire* to go back to a more disciplined routine. That character's conflicting impulses to lethargy and constructive activity are echoed in this one's alternating beliefs. Between bouts of sinking into heaviness, he believes in an interior paradise, a lake surrounded by white mountains gilded with sunlight. But he is frightened of disappearing. Listening or looking attentively at the room or out of the window, he has the impression that a long series of slight, almost imperceptible earthquakes has left the world very fragile.

The first revolutionary episode is presented subjectively, with no realistic description of the rioting in the streets. After he has tried to arbitrate, interrogating the people he sees fighting for their liberty in the Place de la Révolution and remarking on the beatific appearance of the victims, an old man tells him that what he thought he was witnessing took place two centuries ago.

A sexual episode ensues, when a waitress offers herself to him and moves into his flat. "It was very pleasant in the morning to see her naked breasts in the sunlight." But the female sex organ has always seemed to him to be "something like a whirlpool but most of all like an open wound, enormous, incurable, deep." He lets her go on working at the restaurant where he regularly eats, but he is feverishly excited at lying down beside her. "Love was like a jetty into the abyss, a form of despair, a way of dying while accepting death."[6]

When she decides to leave him, there is an awkward attempt to project the disparity between them into dialogue. She complains that without being mad he behaves as though he is. His complaint is that she is never astonished at finding herself in the restaurant or in the street or opposite him. Having lost her innocent eye, she finds nothing strange in all that. Her answer is that she'd hoped her presence would cure him of his malady. He asks what malady, but after carrying her suitcases downstairs and hailing a taxi for her, his last question is who will serve him now in the restaurant. Afterward, like the narrator in *The Mire*, he is uncertain whether he has really lived through what he remembers.

Next comes another revolutionary episode. Ionesco tries to represent the viewpoint of the revolutionaries through the clichés they talk, and he takes some satirical pleasure in showing up the bourgeois habits and attitudes under their subversive activity. One man wants to lunch at home with his wife and then have a rest before returning at 3 o'clock to his barricade. But Ionesco's main point, once again, is to explain their aggressiveness as an outlet for the resentment that has accumulated in them against the human condition. They are killing themselves in each other because they are trying to kill death.

We are again reminded of *The Mire* toward the end of *The Hermit* when time seems to be rushing past at an unknowable rate. The narrative picks up some of the threads from the beginning by referring back to the office, but now he can no longer remember his former colleagues' names. Like *The Mire*, the book ends with a qualified and ambiguous optimism. Probably the narrator is giving an account of the moments of consciousness immediately preceding his death when he describes the tree that abruptly appears outside his window and abruptly vanishes. We are reminded of his theory about almost imperceptible earthquakes and the fragility of the world by the manifestation that follows. The walls and roofs dematerialize, and a desert stretches to the horizon under the luminous sky. A silver ladder seems to descend from just below the sun, and he is surrounded by a garden. When all this disappears again, some of the bright light remains. The final words are "I took that for a sign."[7]

In adapting the novel for the stage, as in making the film *La vase*, Ionesco translates mental processes into dialogue and external events, and, swinging to the opposite extreme from detailing the moment-to-moment consciousness of his Character, he makes him abnormally taciturn. In the first scene he does not speak at all, in the second and third he has scarcely more than one monosyllabic line. The next five scenes consist almost entirely of five monologues to which he listens. Particularly in the first half of the play, all the main statements are made through the minor characters, who are used both to embody modes of life that he rejects and as mouthpieces for ideas that his silence prevents him from expressing.

Very little interaction is possible, and Ionesco identifies only superficially with the characters he is exploiting so inconsistently. He caricatures them in the process of making them reveal themselves in confessional monologues, and he transplants ideas of his own into their alien brains. The first three scenes contain the least theorizing and the most comedy. The play opens in the office, where the boss and the other employees are all reviling the Character, who is about to leave, and the moment he comes in, they all switch to enthusiastic friendliness. The theatrical possibilities of silence as a catalyst are developed most effectively in the second scene, when Lucienne, the woman who has abandoned the Character for a more extravert clerk, tries to win back his confidence, insisting that it isn't his money that interests her. His isolation isolates her: without being able to gauge whether she is boring him or reviving his interest in her, she talks on and on until she is contradicting herself. As in the film version of *The Mire*, Ionesco absorbs phrases from the original narrative into the dialogue. Here, Lucienne is given the line about interior grey spaces full of rubble.

Jacques Dupont, a character who has very little importance in the novel, is built up in the play into an extreme leftist who dominates the third scene, accusing the Character of being politically responsible for the society they are living in, but also indulging in sentimental protestations of camaraderie. His insistence that it must mean something when two men go on working together for thirteen or fifteen years makes the opposite point—that the significance is not proportionate to the time. The joke about his uncertainty whether it is thirteen or fifteen years is repeated too often, and whereas the novel tells us that the narrator's mother had found him the job he had kept ever since, Jacques Mauclair, who was born in 1919 and played the Character in the Paris production of 1973, looked very much older than the character in the novel. There is no explicit reference in the play to his age, but the early retirement and the sexual privation would both make more impact if the Character were still in his thirties.

The five monologues are delivered by the lady who sells the Character his apartment, a dog-owning lady who lives in the same block, her long-suffering husband, a white-haired gentleman, and the concierge. The Character's unresponsiveness is of no catalytic help to their monologues as it was with Lucienne's. Ignoring it, they all go on at great length, unrealistically confiding in him and confessing intimate secrets. Already the style of the play has changed—as it will go on changing—and the flickers of insight and of comedy are insufficient to justify the length of these five speeches, which are used partly to put across Ionesco's own ideas. The white-haired gentleman, for instance, says that whoever created the world did it badly. "We're obliged to eat; we live in a closed economy. Nothing comes to us from outside, and to survive we have to eat each other." He has therefore tried to extinguish all desire in himself, he says. Perhaps we are intended to infer that this is what the Character has done, and the suggestion, which remains undeveloped, is our only clue to the process that made him into what he is. In the novel it was natural for us to accept him unquestioningly because everything was filtered through his consciousness; presented with the appearance on stage of a silent man in his fifties, we are more liable to be curious about his past.

Together the five monologues take up nearly a sixth of the play without carrying the action any further. We then move to the restaurant where the Character eats twice a day, and it is here that we are presented with a mystical sequence that reminds us of the theatrical tricks of A *Stroll in the Air*. The intention is to indicate a change in the level of existence. The staff and the customers in the restaurant are all uplifted—suddenly they are moving in a stylized way—but soon they sink back to their normal level. Then comes the revolutionary sequence. The customers all become revolutionaries, underlining the point made in the novel about the bedrock of bourgeois habit beneath insurrectionary violence. When one of the rebels insults Agnès, the waitress, the Character chivalrously leaps to her defense, and it is after this that she offers herself to him. (In the novel it was two different waitresses and the affair preceded the suburban revolution.)

The affair was also much briefer, occupying only eight out of 182 pages. In the play it is spread over 33 out of 128. The relationship is unconvincingly written, and Geneviève Fontanel, the actress in the Paris production who cleverly doubled the part with Lucienne, was unable to make it credible that she would stay with the Character so long, not because of Jacques Mauclair's age but because there was no substantiation of the non-relationship between them. Nor was there even any genuine desire to explore the relationship, which could have been made interesting and theatrically valid if only its nullity had been brought into focus. Ionesco was right to make the conversation between them minimal, but it seemed artificial when the Character was communicating with her by nodding, shaking his head, or shrugging his shoulders. When he finally spoke, it was to describe the people in the restaurant by saying "They might have been in transparent coffins" and to answer the question of what he wants by saying "I'd like to move the sun." The scene never came to life, and while it was easy enough to sympathize with an attractive, warm-hearted girl faced with indifference, it was hard to sympathize with the Character as much as Ionesco wanted and needed us to if the play was to work.

Nor is there any organic connection between the non-love scenes and the other sequences and speeches that are interwoven with them. The concierge is used as a mouthpiece for Ionesco's belief that while all regimes are bad, revolution serves no purpose. She reiterates the points previously expressed via the white-haired gentleman about the evils of living in a closed economy, where killing is the unavoidable consequence of having to find food in order to survive.

After Agnès has left, time starts to pass at a different speed, as it did toward the end of the novel and of *The Mire*. Within one speech the concierge has delivered the two bottles of brandy that Agnès has bought on her way out, handed over a postcard from her, brought news that she is in the south with her fiancé. Meanwhile the decor is beginning to disappear. The concierge removes some of the furniture, the walls are replaced by scrims, the stage is being prepared for a mystical ending, as in the novel. But before the manifestation of the tree, there are brief sequences with Agnès's daughter (Geneviève Fontanel again) and the sons of many of the characters we have met, all saying how fond their fathers were of the Character. His reaction is hostile, but when he has driven them all out, he is alone on a bare stage, with no concierge to bring him breakfast. Unlike the novel, the play ends with a fit of laughing. The Character now sees everything as a huge joke. He should have realized earlier what it was, and taken less trouble.

# IONESCO'S ACHIEVEMENT

      Looking at the totality of Ionesco's work as
a playwright, it is clear that its importance rests not on
the verbal arabesques he created out of illogicality and
contradiction, but on what he has done to demonstrate
that visually the medium is more flexible than had been
realized. He has minted some of the most striking
images of the postwar theater—the empty chairs that
crowd the stage as a lonely old couple chatters with
invisible guests; the expanding corpse that sprouts
mushrooms as it occupies more and more space in the
apartment and in the consciousness of a married couple;
the proliferating furniture that fills another apartment
as a new tenant tries to move in; the invisible, chuckling
killer who terrorizes a utopian city and, without even
talking, confutes an opponent well armed with liberal
arguments; the manic conformism that dehumanizes
the entire population of a town into a herd of rhinoceroses. All these images can be translated into intel-
lectual "meanings" and they would have less theatrical
resonance if they could not, but it is a mistake to

approach Ionesco in terms of ideas. As a thinker he is undistinguished; his originality is as a theatrical thinker, a writer whose exploration of the medium's potentialities is inseparable from his development of his own ideas. The contrast that recurs in so many plays between visionary euphoria and depressive gloom becomes interesting because of his ability to translate it into lighting effects and movements—as when Bérenger flies. Ionesco's theater, like Shakespeare's, depends less on decor than on pictures created in the audience's mind by words and by deployment of the actors.

It may at first seem puzzling that such a richly visual theater should develop out of a play created from phrases in a language textbook.* But if *Jacques* represents an advance on *The Lesson,* the development was not a mere matter of "coming to understand that dialogue is only a small part of drama." In the conversational clichés of *The Bald Soprano* is a savage satire that mingles uneasily with affectionate amusement at the "typically English" family. An explosion occurs at the end of the play when the tension is released, and it carries on into *The Lesson,* which displays less of the ambivalence and more of the violence in Ionesco's antipathy to language itself and the use that is made of it. A word becomes a lethal weapon as the pontificating teacher uses it to rape and then to kill his defenseless pupil. The play prefigures Peter Handke's *Kaspar,* which

> consists primarily of sentence games and sentence models dealing with the impossibility of expressing anything in language—in other words, of saying something that goes beyond the particular sentence into the realm of significance, mean-

* See page 17 of this volume.

ing. I think a sentence doesn't mean something else: it means itself . . . In constantly pretending to express something, it expresses nothing but its own stupidity.[1]

In *Jacques*, Ionesco's next play after *The Lesson*, the language of common sense is routed by the teeming profusion of organic animality. This prepares the way for the theatrical poetry of his more inspired images. His characters continue to be loquacious, but he is making his theatrical statements through objects, movements, changes of rhythm, stage pictures, modulations of lightning and mood.

Many of his images emerge out of his dreams and fantasies, but then many of his private obsessions are with public issues. His moments of greatest resonance are achieved by amplifying the throb of personal anxiety into an engine-roar of theatricality. Defending Baudelaire against a French critic, Pierre Flottes, who complained that he had never ventured beyond the frontiers of his personality, the English poet Edgell Rickword pointed out that this was not a shortcoming but a virtue he shared with Shakespeare. "To be able to absorb in the products of one's own senses the extrasensual emotions with which, as human beings, we are both burdened and endowed, is the peculiar function of the artist, and it is on the complications of the personality that the richness and variety of the achievement depend."[2] Unlike Pinter's or Albee's, Ionesco's art constantly brings us back to his personality. Plays like *The Killer* and *Rhinoceros* shuttle us between the private nightmare and the political marketplace with such alarming speed that we confuse one with the other, while Ionesco, standing by like a conjuror, transforms our confusion into a revelation.

But he is not a technician. At its inspired best,

Ionesco's theatrical technique seems highly accomplished, but in fact he is improvising devices to meet the needs of the moment. He meets them so generously that he has to ignore the needs of the moments that are likely to come next. His construction, in other words, is one of his weakest points. In his one-act plays a single impulse may carry him from beginning to end, but there is no strong architectural concept to unify the full-length plays. *Exit the King,* with its relentless movement towards death, comes closest to stylistic coherence.

The plays he has produced since his three years of silence (1959–61) are generally inferior to their predecessors: either he stopped because he had lost impetus or failed to regain what he lost by stopping. He is no longer sufficiently disgusted with words to prevent his characters from indulging in rambling expositions of his own ideas. But it would have been difficult, in any event, for him to surpass his achievement of the decade 1948–58. Most younger playwrights have still not caught up with it.

# STAGE AND
# BROADCAST PRODUCTIONS

| | |
|---|---|
| May 1950 | *La cantatrice chauve* (*The Bald Soprano*) directed by Nicholas Bataille who played Mr. Martin himself, at the Théâtre des Noctambules. |
| February 1951 | *La leçon* (*The Lesson*) directed by Marcel Cuvelier, who played the Professor himself, at the Théâtre de Poche. |
| April 1952 | *Les chaises* (*The Chairs*), directed by Sylvain Dhomme, who played the Orator himself, with Paul Chevalier and Tsilla Chelton as the old couple, at the Théâtre Lancry. |
| 1952 | *Le salon de l'automobile* (*The Motor Show*) produced as a radio play. |
| February 1953 | *Victimes du devoir* (*Victims of Duty*), directed by Jacques Mauclair, who played the Detective himself, with R. J. Chauffard as Choubert and Tsilla Chelton as |

Madeleine, at the Théâtre du Quartier Latin.

February 1953    *La jeune fille à marier* (*Maid to Marry*), *Le maître* (*The Leader*), and *Le salon de l'automobile* (*The Motor Show*) produced in a program of seven sketches by Ionesco directed by Jacques Poliéri at the Théâtre de la Huchette.

April 1954    *Amédée ou comment s'en débarasser* (*Amédée or How to Get Rid of It*), directed by Jean-Marie Serreau, with Lucien Raimbourg as Amédée, at the Théâtre de Babylone.

1955    Première in Finland of a Swedish translation of *Le nouveau locataire* (*The New Tenant*), directed by Vivica Bandler.

October 1955    *Jacques ou la soumission* (*Jacques or Obedience*) and *Le tableau* (*The Picture*), directed by Robert Postec, at the Théâtre de la Huchette, with Jean-Louis Trintignant as Jacques.

February 1956    *l'impromptu d'Alma ou le caméléon du berger* (*Improvisation or The Shepherd's Chameleon*), directed by Maurice Jacquemont, who played Ionesco himself, at the Studio des Champs Elysées.

November 1956    *The Bald Soprano* and *The New Tenant*, directed by Peter Wood at the Arts Theatre, London.

May 1957    *The Chairs*, directed by Tony Richardson, at the Royal Court Theatre, London, with Joan Plowright and George Devine.

June 1957    *L'avenir est dans les oeufs ou il faut tout pour faire un monde* (*The Future Is in Eggs or It Takes All*

*Sorts to Make a World*), directed by Jean-Luc Magneron, at the Théâtre de la Cité Universitaire.

September 1957    *Le nouveau locataire* (*The New Tenant*), directed by Robert Postec, with Paul Chevalier, at the Théâtre d'Aujord'hui (French première).

January 1958    *The Chairs* and *The Lesson*, directed by Tony Richardson, at the Phoenix Theatre, New York, with Eli Wallach, Joan Plowright, Max Adrian, and Paula Bauersmith.

June 1958    *The Lesson*, directed by Tony Richardson, at the Royal Court Theatre, London.

March 1959    *Tueur sans gages* (*The Killer*), directed by José Quaglio, with Claude Nicot as Bérenger, at the Théâtre Récamier.

June 1959    *Scène à quatre* (*Foursome*) premièred at the Spoleto Festival.

August 1959    *Rhinoceros* broadcast on BBC Third Programme (first performance).

October 1959    *Die Nashörner* (*Rhinoceros*) directed by Karl Heinz Stroux at the Schauspielhaus, Düsseldorf (world première).

January 1960    *Rhinocéros*, directed by Jean-Louis Barrault, who played Bérenger himself, at the Odéon.

March 1960    *The New Tenant* and *The Lesson*, Directed by Steve Chernak, at the Royal Playhouse, New York.

March 1960    *The Killer*, directed by Richard Barr, at the Seven Arts Theatre, New York.

April 1960    *Apprendre à marcher* (*Learning to Walk*), ballet with scenario by Ionesco, and choreography by

Deryk Mendel, at the Théâtre de l'Etoile.

April 1960    *Rhinoceros*, directed by Orson Welles, with Laurence Olivier as Bérenger, at the Royal Court Theatre, London.

January 1961    *Rhinoceros*, directed by Joseph Anthony, with Eli Wallach, Zero Mostel, and Anne Jackson, at the Longacre Theatre, New York.

February 1962    *The Killer*, directed by Richard Barr, at The Cherry Lane Theatre, New York.

April 1962    *Délire a deux . . . tant qu'on veut* (*Frenzy for Two or More*), directed by Antoine Bourseiller, at the Studio des Champs Elysées.

December 1962    *Le roi se meurt* (*Exit the King*), directed by Jacques Mauclair, who played Bérenger I himself, at the Théâtre de l'Alliance Française.

December 1962    *Der Fussgänger in der Luft* (*A Stroll in the Air*) premièred at the Schauspielhaus, Düsseldorf.

February 1963    *Le piéton de l'air* (*A Stroll in the Air*), directed by Jean-Louis Barrault, who played Bérenger himself, with Madeleine Renaud as Josephine, at the Odéon (French première).

August 1963    *Exit the King,* directed by George Devine, with Alec Guinness, at the Royal Court Theatre, London.

September 1963    *The Bald Soprano* and *The Lesson*, directed by John Nisbet Clark, at the Gate Theater, New York.

March 1964    *Le piéton de l'Air* (*A Stroll in the Air*), directed by Jean-Louis Barrault, at the New York City Center.

| | |
|---|---|
| May 1964 | *The New Tenant* and *Victims of Duty*, directed by Michael Kahn, with Charlotte Rae, Anthony Holland, and Michael Howard, at the Writer's Stage, New York. |
| December 1964 | *Hunger und Durst* (*Hunger and Thirst*) premiered at the Schauspielhaus, Düsseldorf. |
| 1965 | *La lacune* (*The Oversight*) premiered at the Centre Dramatique de Sud-Est, then |
| February 1966 | Revived at the Odéon, Théâtre de France, directed by Jean-Louis Barrault, with Pierre Bertin and Madeleine Renaud. |
| February 1966 | *La soif et la faim* (*Hunger and Thirst*), directed by Jean-Marie Serreau, with Robert Hirsch as Jean, at the Comédie Française, Paris (French première). |
| February 1966 | *La lacune* (*The Oversight*), directed by Jean-Louis Barrault, at the Odéon, Paris. |
| November 1966 | *Pour préparer un oeuf dur* ("how to cook a hard-boiled egg"), directed by Georges Vitaly in a program of ten sketches entitled *Melées et demelées* ("muddles and quarrels"), at the Théâtre de la Bruyère, Paris. The other nine sketches included *Le salon de l'automobile, La jeune fille à marier, Scène à quatre,* and *Le tableau.* |
| January 1968 | *Exit the King,* directed by Ellis Rabb, with Eva Le Galienne and Richard Easton, at the Lyceum Theater, New York. |
| March 1968 | *Victims of Duty* (as one of three one-act plays) directed by Charles |

Fischer, at the East 74th Street Theatre, New York.

January 1970     *Das grosse Massakerspiel* (*Killing Game*), directed by Karl Heinz Stroux and Frantisek Miska, at the Schauspielhaus, Düsseldorf (world première).

September 1970     *Jeux de massacre* (*Killing Game*), directed by Jorge Lavelli, at the Théâtre de Montparnasse, Paris.

1970     *Inédits Ionesco* ("unpublished plays by Ionesco"), directed by Jean Rougerie as a late-night show for Productions d'Aujourd'hui in Paris, then at the Edinburgh Festival, and then in London at the Royal Court's Theatre Upstairs. A program of sketches including *Les salutations*, (*Salutations*), *Scène à Quatre* (*Foursome*), *La lacune* (*The Oversight*), *La jeune fille à marier* (*Maid to Marry*), and *Le maître* (*The Leader*).

February 1972     *Macbett*, directed by Jacques Mauclair, who played Macbett himself, with Geneviève Fontanel, at the Théâtre Rive Gauche, Paris.

July 1973     *Macbett*, directed by Charles Marowitz, with Harry H. Corbett and Frances Cuka, at the Bankside Globe Playhouse.

November 1973     *Ce formidable bordel!* (*What a Hell of a Mess!*), directed by Jacques Mauclair, who played the Character himself, with Geneviève Fontanel, at the Théâtre Moderne, Paris.

April 1974     *Exit the King*, directed by Jacques Mauclair, at the American Place Theatre, New York.

# NOTES

### THE BALD SOPRANO

1. Claude Bonnefoy, ed., *Conversations with Eugène Ionesco* (London: Faber and Faber, 1970), p. 61.
2. *Ibid.*, p. 109.
3. Eugène Ionesco, *Notes and Counter Notes* (London: Calder and Boyars, 1964), p. 95. Published in the United States by Grove Press, 1964.
4. Richard N. Coe, *Ionesco: A Study of His Plays*, rev. ed. (London: Methuen, 1971), p. 12. Translation of first French edition published in the United States as *Eugène Ionesco: A Study of His Work* by Grove Press, 1968.
5. Eugène Ionesco, *Notes and Counter Notes*, p. 136.
6. *Ibid.*, pp. 91–92.
7. *Ibid.*, p. 95.
8. Claude Bonnefoy, ed., *Conversations*, p. 51.
9. *Ibid.*, p. 108.

### THE LESSON

1. Claude Bonnefoy, ed., *Conversations with Eugène Ionesco* (London: Faber and Faber, 1970), p. 165.
2. Eugène Ionesco, *Présent passé passé présent* (Paris: Mercure de France, 1968), p. 26. Published in the

United States as *Present Past, Past Present,* by Grove Press, 1971.

3. Eugène Ionesco, *Notes and Counter Notes* (London: Calder and Boyars, 1964), p. 24.

## JACQUES OR OBEDIENCE AND THE FUTURE IS IN EGGS

1. Eugène Ionesco, *Notes and Counter Notes* (London: Calder and Boyars, 1964), p. 201.
2. *Ibid.,* p. 135.
3. Richard N. Coe, *Ionesco: A Study of His Plays,* rev. ed. (London: Methuen; 1971), p. 71.
4. Claude Bonnefoy, ed., *Conversations with Eugène Ionesco* (London: Faber and Faber, 1970), p. 136.
5. Richard Schechner, "Eugène Ionesco," in *On Contemporary Literature,* ed. Richard Kostelanetz (Avon: Discus Books, 1964).

## THE CHAIRS

1. Claude Bonnefoy, ed., *Conversations with Eugène Ionesco* (London: Faber and Faber, 1970), pp. 72–73.
2. *Ibid.,* p. 96.
3. Eugène Ionesco, *Notes and Counter Notes* (London: Calder and Boyars, 1964), p. 200.
4. *Ibid.,* p. 197.

## VICTIMS OF DUTY

1. Claude Bonnefoy, ed., *Conversations with Eugène Ionesco* (London: Faber and Faber, 1970), p. 97.
2. Eugène Ionesco, *Notes and Counter Notes* (London: Calder and Boyars, 1964), p. 276.
3. Claude Bonnefoy, ed., *Conversations,* p. 35.
4. Published as a collection in the United States, *The Colonel's Photograph and Other Stories* (New York: Grove Press, 1969), including: "Oriflamme," "The Colonel's Photograph," "The Stroller in the Air," "A Victim of Duty," "Rhinoceros," "Slough," and "Spring."
5. Eugène Ionesco, *Fragments of a Journal* (London: Faber and Faber, 1968), p. 69. Published in the United States by Grove Press, 1968.
6. Claude Bonnefoy, ed., *Conversations,* pp. 31–32.

## The Motor Show, Maid to Marry, and The Leader

1. As an appendix in Richard N. Coe, *Ionesco: A Study of His Plays*, rev. ed. (London: Methuen, 1971). ed. (London: Methuen, 1971).

## Amédée

1. T. S. Eliot, *Complete Poems & Plays, 1909–1950* (New York: Harcourt Brace Jovanovich, 1952).
2. Claude Bonnefoy, ed., *Conversations with Eugène Ionesco* (London: Faber and Faber, 1970), p. 85.
3. *Ibid.*, p. 83.

## The Picture

1. Leonard Pronko, *Eugène Ionesco* Essays on Modern Writers (New York: Columbia University Press, 1965).

## Rhinoceros

1. Eugène Ionesco, *Présent passé passé présent* (Paris: Mercure de France, 1968), p. 114.
2. *Ibid.*, p. 118.
3. Claude Bonnefoy, ed., *Conversations with Eugène Ionesco* (London: Faber and Faber, 1970), p. 40.
4. Eugène Ionesco, *Notes and Counter Notes* (London: Calder and Boyars, 1964), p. 215.
5. Claude Bonnefoy, ed., *Conversations*, p. 102.

## A Stroll in the Air

1. Claude Bonnefoy, ed., *Conversations with Eugène Ionesco* (London: Faber and Faber, 1970), p. 65.
2. *Ibid.*, p. 65.
3. Richard N. Coe, *Ionesco: A Study of His Plays*, rev. ed. (London: Methuen, 1971), p. 104.
4. Roger Shattuck, ed., *Jarry's Selected Works* (London: Methuen, 1965), p. 192.
5. *Ibid.*, p. 114.

## Exit the King

1. Claude Bonnefoy, ed., *Conversations with Eugène Ionesco* (London: Faber and Faber, 1970), p. 79.
2. *Ibid.*, p. 77.

3. *Ibid.*, pp. 98–99.
4. Eugène Ionesco, *Fragments of a Journal* (London: Faber and Faber, 1968).
5. *Ibid.*, p. 40.

## HUNGER AND THIRST

1. Eugène Ionesco, *Présent passé passé présent* (Paris: Mercure de France, 1968), p. 29.
2. Claude Bonnefoy, ed., *Conversations with Eugène Ionesco* (London: Faber and Faber, 1970), p. 74.
3. Eugène Ionesco, *Présent passé*, p. 180.
4. Simone Benmussa, *Ionesco* Théâtre de tous les temps (Paris: Seghers, 1966).
5. In a discussion with Ionesco published in the *Nouvel Observateur* (February 1966), Jean-Marie Serreau described this brainwashing sequence as Brechtian. Ionesco's answer was that he thought he had written a Zen play, but that if the spectator came out from seeing it a different person from what he was when he went in, then it would have succeeded.

## KILLING GAME

1. This is the date of the first French performance; the American edition bearing this title was not published until 1974.
2. Interview with Ossia Trilling quoted by Tom Bishop in "Ionesco on Olympus," *Saturday Review*, 16 May 1970.

## MACBETT

1. Jan Kott, *Shakespeare Our Contemporary* (New York: Doubleday, 1965).
2. (Paris, 3 February 1972).

## THE MIRE, THE HERMIT, AND WHAT A HELL OF A MESS!

1. Published in *The Times* (London: 12 February 1974).
2. *Ibid.*
3. *Ibid.*
4. All of these novels and plays are found in *The Collected Works of Samuel Beckett*, 16 vols. (New York: Grove Press, 1970).

5. Eugène Ionesco, *Le solitaire* (Paris: Mercure de France, 1973). Published in the United States as *The Hermit* by Viking Press, 1974.
6. *Ibid.*
7. *Ibid.*

IONESCO'S ACHIEVEMENT
1. Peter Handke, interview in *The Drama Review*, vol. 15, no. 1 (Fall 1970).
2. Edgell Rickword, *Essays and Opinions 1921–31* (Cheshire: Carcanet Press, 1974).

# BIBLIOGRAPHY

TEXTS

In France, Gallimard publishes Ionesco's plays in four volumes:

Théâtre I: *La cantatrice chauve—La leçon—Jacques ou la soumission—Les chaises—Victimes du devoir—Amédée ou comment s'en débarrasser* (1954)

Théâtre II: *L'impromptu de l'Alma—Tueur sans gages—Le nouveau locataire—L'avenir est dans les oeufs—Le maître—La jeune fille à marier* (1958)

Théâtre III: *Rhinocéros—Le piéton de l'air—Délire à deux—Le tableau—Scène à quatre—Les salutations—La colère* (1963)

Théâtre IV: *Le roi se meurt—La soif et la faim—La lacune—Le salon de l'automobile—L'oeuf dur—Pour préparer un oeuf dur—Le jeune homme à marier—Apprende à marcher* (1966).

Published individually in Gallimard's Manteau d'Arlequin collection are *Rhinocéros* (1959), *Le roi se meurt* (1963), *Jeux de massacre* (1970), *Macbett* (1973), *Ce formidable bordel!* (1973). *Les leçons de français pour Americains* is published in the Cahiers Renaud-Barrault No. 54 April 1966. Gallimard also publishes *Notes et* contre-notes (1962), *La photo du colonel* (1962), and *Discours de réception d'Eugène Ionesco a l'Academie française et réponse de Jean Delay* (1971). Mercure de France publishes *Journal en miettes* (1967), *Présent passé passé présent* (1968), and *Le solitaire* (1973). Pierre Belfond publishes *Entretiens avec Claude Bonnefoy* (1966). Skira publishes *Découvertes* (1969).

In Great Britain Calder and Boyars publishes English translations by Donald Watson of most of the plays in eight volumes, not arranged in exact chronological order:
I: *The Chairs—The Bald Prima Donna—The Lesson—Jacques* (1958)
II: *Amédée—The New Tenant—Victims of Duty* (1958)
III: *The Killer—Improvisation—Maid to Marry* (1960)
IV: *Rhinoceros—The Leader—The Future Is in Eggs* (1960)
V: *Exit the King—The Motor Show—Foursome*
VI: *A Stroll in the Air—Frenzy for Two* (1965)
VII: *Hunger and Thirst—The Picture—Anger—Salutation* (1968)
VIII: *Here Comes a Chopper—The Oversight—The Foot of the Wall* (1971)
IX: *Macbett—The Mire—Learning to Walk* (1973)
X: *What a Bloody Circus!—The Hard Boiled Egg* (1975)

Calder and Boyars also publishes *Notes and Counter Notes* (1964) and *Past Present Present Past* (1972). The author and publisher wish to thank Calder and Boyars Ltd. for permission to reprint extracts from these and from the translations of the plays. Faber and Faber publishes *The Colonel's Photograph* (1967), *Fragments of a Journal* (1968), and *Conversations with Eugene Ionesco*, Claude Bonnefoy, ed. 1970). The author and publisher wish to thank Faber and Faber for permission to reprint extracts from these.

In the United States Grove Press publishes most of the plays in English translation:
*Four Plays* (*The Bald Soprano—The Lesson—The Chairs—Jack, or the Submission*), Donald M. Allen, tr. (1958); *Three Plays* (*Amédée—The New Tenant—Victims of Duty*), Donald Watson, tr. (1958); *The Killer and Other Plays* (*Improvisation, or The Shepherd's Chameleon—Maid*

to Marry), Donald Watson, tr. (1960); Rhinoceros and Other Plays (The Leader—The Future Is in Eggs, or It Takes All Sorts to Make a World), Derek Prouse, tr. (1960); Exit the King, Donald Watson, tr. (1967); A Stroll in the Air and Frenzy for Two or More: Two Plays, Donald Watson, tr. (1968); Hunger and Thirst and Other Plays (The Picture—Anger—Salutations), Donald Watson, tr. (1969); Macbett, Charles Marowitz, tr. (1973); Killing Game, Helen Gary Bishop, tr. (1974).

Grove Press also publishes Notes and Counter Notes: Writings on the Theater, Donald Watson, tr. (1964); Fragments of a Journal, Jean Pace, tr. (1968); The Colonel's Photograph and Other Stories, Jean Stewart and John Russell, trs. (1969); Present Past, Past Present, Helen R. Lane, tr. (1971). The Viking Press publishes The Hermit, Richard Seaver, tr. (1974).

### INTERVIEWS

Hayman, Ronald. "A Postscript on Ionesco." Encore No. 14, vol. V (May–June 1958).
Wildman, Carl. "Ionesco Talking." Plays and Players (April 1965).
Wagner, Walter, ed. The Playwrights Speak. London: Longmans Green & Co. (1969).

### SELECTED CRITICISM

Benmussa, Simone. Ionesco. Théâtre de tous les temps. Paris: Seghers, 1966.
Coe, Richard N. Eugène Ionesco. Writers and Critics Series. Edinburgh: Oliver and Boyd, 1961. Rev. ed., Ionesco: A Study of His Plays. London: Methuen, 1971. American rev. ed., Eugène Ionesco: A Study of His Work. New York: Grove Press, 1968.
Donnard, J. H. Ionesco, dramaturge. Paris: Lettres Modernes-Minard, 1966.
Esslin, Martin. The Theatre of the Absurd. London: Eyre and Spottiswoode, 1962. New York: Doubleday, 1969. Brief Chronicles. London: Temple Smith, 1970.
Fletcher, John, ed. Forces of Modern French Drama. London: University of London Press, 1972. New York: Frederick Ungar Publishing Co., 1972.
Grossvogel, David I. Twentieth Century French Drama

(orig. *The Self-Conscious Stage in Modern French Drama*). New York: Columbia University Press, 1961. *The Blasphemers: The Theatre of Brecht, Ionesco, Beckett, Genet*. Ithaca: Cornell University Press, 1965.

Jacobson, Josephine and Mueller, William R. *Ionesco and Genet: Playwrights of Silence*. New York: Hill and Wang, 1968.

Lamont, Rosette C., ed. *Ionesco: A Collection of Critical Essays*. Englewood.Cliffs; Prentice-Hall, 1973.

*L'Avant-Scène*. Special Ionesco Issue. Nos. 373–374.

Lewis, Allan. *Ionesco*. World Authors Series. New York: Twayne Publishers, 1972.

Morris, Kelly, ed. *Genet/Ionesco: The Theater of the Double; A Critical Anthology*. New York: Bantam Books, 1969.

Pronko, Leonard. *Eugène Ionesco*. Essays on Modern Writers. New York: Columbia University Press, 1965.

Schechner, Richard. "Eugène Ionesco" in *On Contemporary Literature*. Edited by Richard Kostelanetz. New York: Avon Books, Discus, 1969.

Serreau, Geneviève. *Histoire du nouveau théâtre*. Collection des Idées. Paris: Gallimard, 1966.

*Tulane Drama Review* 7 (Spring 1963).

Vernois, Paul. *Le dynamique théâtre d'Eugène Ionesco*. Paris: Editions Klincksieck, 1972.

Wendt, Ernst. *Ionesco*. Dramatiker des Welttheaters. Velber: Friedrich Verlag.

Wilbern, Julian H. *Brecht & Ionesco*. Urbana: University of Illinois Press, 1971.

# INDEX

Absurd, Theater of the, 13
Absurd elements, 28, 73, 114
Action, dramatic, 46, 72–73, 155, 164
  in *Amédée*, 78, 80
  in *The Chairs*, 44, 46
  in *Frenzy for Two*, 113, 114
  in *The Killer*, 92, 96
  in *The New Tenant*, 75, 77
Actors
  relationships of, with audience, 67
  use of, 63
  views on, 6, 17, 24
Adaptations, of short stories, 61–62
Agnosticism, 16
Albee, Edward, 187

Alienation effect, 48, 67, 72
Ambiguity, 82, 178
*Amédée*, 5, 25, 78–84, 93, 99, 137, 151
  characterization in, 6
  dialogue in, 105
  ending of, 95
  imagery of flying in, 65, 92
Anachronisms, 152, 165
Antitheater, 33
Art, Croce's views on, 6–7
*Au pied de la mur*, 12n
Authoritarianism, views on, 28, 70
Autobiographical elements, 28, 39, 65–66, 76, 187
  in *Hunger and Thirst*, 137–38, 139
  in *The Killer*, 91, 97

*Bald Soprano, The*, 5, 18–25, 30, 32, 39, 46, 63, 73, 117, 146
   as "antiplay," 33
   characterization in, 26, 170
   illustration, 58–59
   language in, 65, 186
Ballet scenarios, 75, 128
Banality, use of, 7, 17, 18, 22, 35, 36, 72, 86, 178, 186
Barrault, Jean-Louis, 112
Barthes, Roland, 87
Bataille, Nicolas, 5n, 58–59
Baudelaire, Charles, 187
Beckett, Samuel, 44, 172, 175
   *Endgame*, 130
   *Krapp's Last Tape*, 175
   *Malone Dies*, 175
   *Murphy*, 175
Bérenger, 6, 7, 9, 34, 126
   in *Exit the King*, 131
   in *The Killer*, 91–95, 96, 97–100
   in *Rhinoceros*, 104, 105, 109, 111
   in *A Stroll in the Air*, 116, 121, 123–24
Bergson, Henri (quoted), 25
Bonnefoy, Claude, 65, 128, 138
Bosch, Hieronymous, 149
Boulevard theater, 33
Bourgeoisie, portrayal of, 5, 10, 23–24, 33–34, 77, 78, 92, 154, 178, 181
Boys, C. V., 121n
Brecht, Bertolt, 24, 48
   *Puntila*, 64
   *Seven Deadly Sins*, 40
   views on, 28, 89
Breton, André, 13
Buber, Martin, 8–9

Camber, Melinda, 171, 173
Camus, Albert: *La Peste*, 148, 152
Cannibalism, 158
Caricature, 28, 33, 179
*Chairs, The*, 5, 24, 43–52, 61, 63, 64, 66, 75, 83, 84, 143, 149
   action in, 73, 113
   illustration, 54
   themes in, 131, 136
   women in, 10, 66
Characterization, 24, 28–29, 34, 47, 76, 104–105, 131, 147, 174, 177, 179, 187, 188
   in *Amédée*, 79, 82
   in *The Bald Soprano*, 23, 26
   of Bérenger, 91, 104, 116
   in *The Chairs*, 43, 47
   discontinuity of, 62, 68, 70, 86
   and Ionesco as character, 87–90, 170–73, 174
   and Ionesco-like characters, 6, 39, 116
   and Ionesco's mouthpieces, 147, 170, 182

in *Killing Game*, 152,
157, 158
in *The Lesson*, 26–27, 28
in *Macbett*, 163, 164,
165, 167
in *The Picture*, 85
Chauffard, R. J., 63–64
Chorus, 40, 41, 42, 125,
126, 131, 132, 151
Claudel, Paul, 13
*Le soulier de satin*, 12
Clichés. *See* Banality
Climaxes, 70, 73, 80, 81,
83, 95, 113–14, 125,
152
Coe, Richard, 8, 23, 46,
121
*Colonel's Photograph, The*,
65, 95, 115
Comedy, 72, 84, 88, 99,
148, 159, 165, 172
and burlesque elements,
17
and clown show, 160
in *The Hermit*, 179, 180
and jokes, 77, 165, 180
in *The Lesson*, 29, 73
in *Rhinoceros*, 105, 112
Communication, 20–21, 23,
171
Communism, 102
Concierge character, 10, 76,
98, 182
Confessional speeches, 48
Confusion, 19, 30, 34, 92
Contradictions, 8, 19, 21,
44, 45, 48, 72, 179,
185
Contrast, 186

*Conversations with Eugène
Ionesco*, 39
Criticism
and Ionesco's self-criti-
cism, 25, 126
of Ionesco's plays, 8, 24,
115
and satire on critics, 87
Croce, Benedetto, 6

Dadaism, 13
Dance, use of, 39, 41
Death, obsession with, 13–
14, 15–16, 24–25,
35, 66, 68, 154, 173
in *Amédée*, 79, 80
in *The Chairs*, 51
in *Exit the King*, 128–31,
133, 134–35
in *The Future Is in Eggs*,
41
in *The Hermit*, 178
in *The Killer*, 92
in *Killing Game*, 148,
150, 151, 156–57,
158, 159
in *The Lesson*, 27, 31, 32
in *Macbett*, 166
in *A Stroll in the Air*,
125
in *Victims of Duty*, 70
Defoe, Daniel: *The Journal
of the Plague Year*,
148–49, 151–52
Descartes, René, 9
Dialogue, 5, 44
in *Amédée*, 78

Dialogue (*cont'd*)
  in *The Bald Soprano*, 22, 26
  in *The Chairs*, 48
  in *The Future Is in Eggs*, 40–41, 42
  in *Improvisation*, 87, 89
  in *Jacques or Obedience*, 34–35, 38, 40
  in *The Killer*, 93
  in *Killing Game*, 150–51, 155, 156
  in *The Leader*, 73
  in *The Lesson*, 29, 31
  in *Macbett*, 164
  in *The Motor Show*, 71–72
  in *The New Tenant*, 75
  in *Rhinoceros*, 105, 107
  in *A Stroll in the Air*, 118, 119–20, 126
  in *Victims of Duty*, 67
Diary, 101, 102, 103
Didacticism, 32
Dogma, views on, 28, 89
Dort, Bernard, 87
Dostoevsky, Feodor: *The Possessed*, 5n, 15
Dramatic devices, 28, 72–73, 181, 188. *See also* Stage effects
Dreams, 9–10, 77, 146, 187
  in *Hunger and Thirst*, 138, 139
  in *The Killer*, 92–93, 94, 95
  in *Killing Game*, 153–54
  in *A Stroll in the Air*, 116, 117, 125

Educational system, criticism of, 10
Eliot, T. S.
  *The Family Reunion*, 151
  *The Wasteland*, 78, 80
Endings
  of *Amédée*, 84
  of *The Bald Soprano*, 26
  of *The Chairs*, 52
  of *Jacques or Obedience*, 38–39
  of *The Lesson*, 32
  of *Macbett*, 168
  of *Victims of Duty*, 70
English, learning of, 17
Epic theater, 89
Exaggeration, 28
Existentialism, 8n, 16
*Exit the King*, 11, 75, 116, 128–36, 152, 164, 165, 188
  illustration, 57, 60
Externalization technique, 64–65

Fantasy, 96, 101, 187
Farce, 69, 111
  and tragedy, 160, 164
Fascism, 32, 101
Feydeau, Georges: *A Flea in Her Ear*, 25
Films, 6, 169–70, 171, 172, 173, 179
Flottes, Pierre, 187
Fontanel, Geneviève, 181, 182
*Foot of the Wall, The*, 12n
*Fragments of a Journal*, 9, 13, 35, 39, 129

*Frenzy for Two*, 46, 113–14, 137
Freud, Sigmund, views on, 10
*Future Is in Eggs, The*, 33, 36, 40–42, 75

Game-playing element, 8,10
Gauthier, Jean-Jacques, 87
Ghosts
  in *Hunger and Thirst*, 139–40
  in *Macbett*, 167
Giraudoux, Jean: *L'improvisation de Paris*, 87
Grand Guignol, 24
*Grandes chaleurs, Les*, 71
Greek drama, 11
Grotesque, the, 28, 39, 45

Handke, Peter: *Kaspar*, 186
Hasidism, 8–9n
Heisenberg, Werner, 123
*Hermit, The*, 169, 174–83
Humanism, 108
*Hunger and Thirst*, 11, 12, 15, 137–47, 158
  characterization in, 157, 170
  and stage effects, 165
  women in, 10

Ibsen, Henrik, 142
  settings of, 77
Ideology
  in drama, 7
  of Ionesco, 186
Imagery, 65–66, 82, 126, 127, 131, 161, 175, 185, 187

cosmic, 132, 165
of flying and elevation, 65, 66, 68, 92, 116, 123–24, 126, 173
of light, 82
of mud, 65, 66, 139, 172–73
visual, 141
of weight and weightlessness, 65, 79, 82, 84, 105
*Improvisation*, 87–90, 126, 127
Improvisational technique, 188
*Inédits Ionesco*, 74
Intermissions, and dramatic structure, 11–12, 81, 158–59
Ionesco, Eugène
  acting career of, 5–6
  and Bérenger, 116
  as character, 87–90, 170–73, 174
  childhood and youth of, 14, 35, 76, 137–38
  father of, 28, 137–38
  interview with, 5–16
  mystical experience of, 97
  on theater, 64
  theatrical career of, 115, 185–88
  and World War II, 102
Irrelevance, 167

*Jacques or Obedience*, 5, 33–40, 186, 187
  as ballet, 75

*Jacques or Obedience*
  (*cont'd*)
  dreams in, 146
  imagery in, 65
  and language, 63
  themes of, 51
*Jacques* plays, 33
Japanese Noh Theater, 11
Jarry, Alfred
  *The Exploits and Opin-
    ions of Dr. Faus-
    troll, 'Pataphysician*,
    122
  "How to Construct a
    Time Machine,"
    122–23
  influence of, 7, 24, 121–23
  "The Passion Considered
    as an Uphill Bicycle
    Race," 124
  *Ubu Roi*, 27–28, 85,
    160–61
Jean, as Ionesco's mouth-
    piece, 147
Jean Rougerie Company, 74
Jung, Carl, 9, 10, 96

Kafka, Franz, 91
  *Metamorphoses*, 103
Kelvin, Lord, 121n
*Killer, The*, 11, 91–100,
    104, 111, 138, 187
  and Bérenger, 116
  characterization in, 131
  dialogue in, 105
  imagery in, 65
  themes in, 146
*Killing Game*, 11, 148–59
  characterization in, 170

and death theme, 166
  imagery in, 161
Kott, Jan: *Shakespeare Our
    Contemporary*, 161

Language, 33, 185, 188
  in *The Bald Soprano*,
    17–20, 22, 23
  in *The Chairs*, 50
  from conversation
    manual, 17, 33
  and games, 10–11
  Ionesco on, 171
  in *Jacques*, 38, 187
  in *The Lesson*, 29–31, 32,
    186
  in *The New Tenant*, 76
  in *The Picture*, 86
  and pseudotechnical
    vocabulary, 72
  and verbal patterning,
    164
  in *Victims of Duty*, 67,
    68
  *See also* Dialogue;
    Wordplay
*Leader, The*, 72–73
Le Corbusier's *ville
    radieuse*, 91
*Les connaissez-vous?*, 71
*Lesson, The*, 11, 26–32, 70,
    146, 186, 187
  characterization in, 34,
    47, 89, 169
  language in, 38, 86
  women in, 10
Lighting, stage, 186, 187
  of *Exit the King*, 129
  of *The Killer*, 93, 96

Love, Ionesco on, 173–74, 177

*Macbett*, 160–68, 170
*Maid to Marry*, 72, 85
Malapropisms, 34, 35
Mao Tse-tung's *Red Book*, 14
Marriage theme, 40, 51, 72, 73, 114
Masks, use of, 34
Mauclair, Jacques, 54, 57, 63, 68, 180, 181
Melodrama, parody of, 22
Message, in drama, 8, 10, 12, 88
Metaphors, 104
Metaphysics, 9, 121
Militarism, views on, 28
Miller, Arthur: *Death of a Salesman*, 93–94
Mime, 47, 75
*Mire, The*, 169, 174, 176–77, 178, 179, 182
Molière's *L'improvisation de Versailles*, 87
Monologue, 29, 85, 111, 140, 142, 179, 180, 181
Montage technique, 118
Motifs, 39
*Motor Show, The*, 71–72, 73
Moulnier, Emmanuel, 8
Movement, theatrical, 62, 70, 80, 83, 186, 187
"Mud," 65
Music and song, use of, 35, 63, 83, 98, 118, 126, 156–57, 167
Mystical element, 181

Nabokov, Vladimir, 8
Names, use of, 34
Narrator, 61–62, 176
Nazism, 14, 15, 101, 102, 103, 109, 135, 146
Nerval, Gérard de: *Promenades et souvenirs*, 52
*New Tenant, The*, 75–77
  action in, 80, 113
  dialogue in, 78
  movement in, 83
*Nièce-épouse, La*, 71
Nihilism, 116
Nonsense
  in *The Bald Soprano*, 18, 22
  in *The Chairs*, 45
  in *Jacques*, 35
  in *The Killer*, 98
  in *Killing Game*, 156
  in *The Lesson*, 29, 30
  in *The Picture*, 86
Nostalgia, 64, 173
*Notes and Counter Notes*, 13, 23, 95, 111
Nothingness, 43–44, 136
Novels, 169, 179, 181

Optimism, 178
*Oriflamme*, 79, 81, 82, 83, 95

Parallelism, 155
Parody, 22, 33, 165
'Pataphysics, 7–8, 121, 123

Personalism, 8
Philology, study of, 11
*Picture, The*, 85–86
Pinter, Harold, 21, 187
Pirandello, Luigi, 7
Poetry, in plays, 22, 38, 63
Poincaré, Lucien, 10
Poirot-Delpech, Bertrand, 161
Polier, Jacques, 71
Political themes, 15, 146, 187
    in *The Hermit*, 178
    in *The Killer*, 91
    in *Killing Game*, 156
    in *The Lesson*, 32
    in *Rhinoceros*, 101, 103–104
    in *Victims of Duty*, 62
Politics, views on, 14, 99
Postec, Robert, 129
*Présent passé passé présent*, 28, 29n, 96, 108, 137–38
Prévert, Jacques, 7n
Progression, in drama, 11
Proliferation, 25, 185
    in *Amédée*, 80
    in *The Chairs*, 49
    in *Exit the King*, 136
    in *Frenzy for Two*, 113–14
    in *The Future Is in Eggs*, 42
    in *Hunger and Thirst*, 146
    in *Killing Game*, 150
    in *The New Tenant*, 75, 76, 77

in Shakespeare, 161
    in *Victims of Duty*, 69–70
Pronko, Leonard, 85
Puns, 22–23, 69, 165
Puppet-show tradition, 17, 132
    and characterization, 63, 150

Queneau, Raymond, 7n

Racine, Jean Baptiste, 11
Radio plays, 71
Realism, 95
Recognition scene, 22
Religion, views on, 10, 16, 119, 121
    and religious theme, 146
Repetition, 164
Revolution, views on, 174, 181
*Rhinoceros*, 26, 101–112, 114, 116, 156, 187
    characterization in, 34, 47
    illustration, 53
*Rhume onirique, Le*, 71
Rhythm, 46, 151, 175, 187
    in *The Bald Soprano*, 20, 25
    in *Exit the King*, 129
    in *The Future Is in Eggs*, 40–41, 42
    in *Jacques*, 37, 38, 40
    in *The Lesson*, 31
Rickword, Edgell, 187

Sartre, Jean-Paul, 16
Satire, 23, 40, 67, 72–73, 87, 186

in *The Hermit*, 178
in *Rhinoceros*, 105
in *Victims of Duty*, 62
Schneider, Gerard, 64
Setting, 5
  in *The Chairs*, 44, 45
  in *The Killer*, 98
  in *Killing Game*, 149,
    150, 155
Sexuality, 26, 31, 32, 38,
  48, 62, 177
Shakespeare, William, 186,
  187
  *As You Like It*, 162
  ideology of, 7
  influence of, 131, 132,
    133
  *Julius Caesar*, 132
  *Macbeth*, 13, 132, 160,
    161, 163, 164, 165–
    66, 167
  *The Tempest*, 162
Shattuck, Roger, 121n
Short stories, 61, 65, 79,
  95, 103, 104, 115,
  120–21, 169, 174
Silence, dramatic use of,
  20, 48, 179
Social themes, 8, 24, 93,
  97. *See also* Bour-
  geoisie, portrayal of
Soliloquy, 99
Solitude, 68, 169, 171
  Ionesco on, 15, 23
Sound effects
  in *Amédée*, 80
  in *The Chairs*, 44, 49, 51
  in *The Killer*, 93
  in *The Leader*, 72

in *The Motor Show*, 71–
  72
in *Rhinoceros*, 105, 106
Soupault, Philippe, 13
Stage effects, 37–38, 44, 187
  in *Amédée*, 80, 83–84
  in *The Chairs*, 49
  in *Jacques*, 40
  in *The Killer*, 94, 96
  in *Macbett*, 165, 167–68
  in *The New Tenant*, 76,
    77
  in *Rhinoceros*, 106
  in *A Stroll in the Air*,
    117–18, 120
  in *Victims of Duty*, 64
  *See also*: Lighting,
    stage; Movement,
    theatrical; Proliferal-
    tion; Sound effects
Stream of consciousness, 13
Strindberg, August, 142
*Stroll in the Air, A*, 7, 8, 9,
  115–27, 157, 158,
    167, 181
  dreams in, 138
  illustration, 56
  imagery in, 65
  rhythm in, 46
  stage effects in, 165
  themes in, 137
Structure of plays, 11–12,
  148, 158–59, 188
Stylization, 105
Subjective attitude, 93, 146
Surreal elements
  in *The Bald Soprano*, 22
  in *The Future Is in Eggs*,
    40

Surreal elements (cont'd)
  in *Jacques*, 36, 37–38
  in *The Lesson*, 28
  in *Maid to Marry*, 72
  in *The Motor Show*, 71
  in *La vase*, 171
Surrealism movement, 12–13
Syllogisms, 105, 114
  and pseudologic, 18, 185
Symbols, 172
  in *Amédée*, 80
  of concierge, 10
  in *The Future Is in Eggs*, 40
  in *The Lesson*, 27, 32

Technique, 104, 107, 158, 187, 188. *See also:* Characterization; Climaxes; Dialogue; Dramatic devices; Imagery; Language; Stage effects; Structure of plays
Themes, 131, 145, 146
  in *Frenzy for Two*, 113
  in *Killing Game*, 150–151
  in *Rhinoceros*, 105
  *See also:* Death, obsession with; Political themes; Social themes
Thriller element, 62, 97, 105
Time, 19
Totalitarianism, 91, 96, 103–104, 116, 145

Toynbee, Philip, 24
Tragedy, 111
  and tragicomedy, 148, 160, 164
Translations, English, 22–23, 36, 84
Tynan, Kenneth, 24

Universe, view of, 174
Utopianism, 96, 143

*Vase, La*, 6, 169–70, 171–74, 179
Viala, Akakia, 5n
Vian, Boris, 7n
*Victims of Duty*, 61–70, 75, 76, 82, 85, 121, 135
  illustration, 55
Violence
  in *Frenzy for Two*, 114
  in *The Hermit*, 181
  in *Killing Game*, 154
  in *The Lesson*, 186
  in *Rhinoceros*, 113
Visual theater, 186
Vitrac, Roger, 13

Welles, Orson, 24, 110
*What a Hell of a Mess!*, 169, 170, 174
Women, views on, 10, 28, 45, 66, 138
Wordplay, 10–11, 29–30, 38, 45
Wordsworth, William: *Intimations of Immortality*, 145

Zen Buddhism, 121